D0351086

The Architect and the City

THE M.I.T. PRESS
Massachusetts Institute of Technology
Cambridge, Massachusetts,
and London, England

The Architect and the City

MARCUS WHIFFEN, EDITOR

Papers from the
AIA-ACSA Teacher Seminar
Cranbrook Academy of Art
June 11–22, 1962

Library of Congress Catalog Card Number: 66-23801
Printed in the United States of America

Cities have often been likened to symphonies and poems, and the comparison seems to me a perfectly natural one: they are, in fact, objects of the same kind. The city may even be rated higher, since it stands at the point where Nature and artifice meet. A city is a congregation of animals whose biological history is enclosed within its boundaries; and yet every conscious and rational act on the part of these creatures helps to shape the city's eventual character. By its form, as by the manner of its birth, the city has elements at once of biological procreation, organic evolution, and aesthetic creation. It is both natural object and a thing to be cultivated; individual and group; something lived and something dreamed; it is *the* human invention, *par excellence*.

Claude Lévi-Strauss, *Tristes Tropiques*,
translated by John Russell (New York: Criterion Books, 1961)

1962 Teacher Seminar Committee Structure

Steering Committee
Harold Bush-Brown, General Chairman
Donald Q. Faragher, Finances
Harlan E. McClure

Scholarship Committee
Harlan E. McClure, Chairman
Karel Yasko
Maurice W. Perreault

Program Committee
Harold Bush-Brown, Chairman
Thomas W. Mackesey, Moderator
Robert H. Snyder
David A. Crane, Consultant
Denise Scott Brown
Joseph J. Schiffer
Maurice W. Perreault, AIA Staff

Norman D. Day, Editor

Edith S. Franchini, Secretary

Foreword

The papers collected here were presented at the seventh annual seminar for teachers of architecture at Cranbrook Academy of Art, Bloomfield Hills, Michigan, in June 1962, held under the joint auspices of the American Institute of Architects and the Association of Collegiate Schools of Architecture.

In an age when science and technology are capable of providing satisfactory conditions for all, we find a man-made physical world that fails to inspire and, for the majority, rarely achieves health, safety, and efficiency. The subject matter of these papers relates to areas of population concentration, hence the title of the seminar, "The Architect and the City."

The seminar's educational theme concerned the enlargement of the scope of objectives beyond the quality of individual buildings to include increased responsibility for the community as a whole. What can and should our schools be doing to meet this problem? There can be no question that the man with the background of a sound education in architecture has an important role to play. To be effective in community planning requires broad interests and understanding in many disciplines.

Harold Bush-Brown, FAIA

Editor's Note

Editing is an occupation without any clear code of practice — or, as some authors might add (*vide* the recent correspondence in the London *Times Literary Supplement*), of ethics. An editor must still, as a rule, decide for himself how he will treat the manuscripts entrusted to his care. (The exceptions occur when their subject matter is drawn from one of those fields which have undergone the process that has been called "scientization," when translation into the special language that may be given the equally inelegant name of "dissertationese" is doubtless mandatory.) The first question is whether to do as much as permissible or as little as needful. The present editor chose the latter course, even to the extent of leaving in references to the local Michigan scene, which meant more to the seminar participants than they may mean to the reader who was not there. After all, these are papers that were written to be delivered, and that were delivered, at a certain place, in a certain company; and it is not inappropriate that the reader should be reminded of this fact occasionally. And then, of course, they were also written to be delivered at a certain time. It may be that some of the contributors have subsequently changed their views about some things, or that they might choose to emphasize different points today. In fairness to them, the reader should be told that although each author was given the opportunity of revising his paper, extensive rewriting and material alterations of sense or content were specifically forbidden him.

Abstracts of the papers, edited by Norman D. Day, were printed in the *Journal of Architectural Education*, Volume XVII, Nos. 2 and 3 (November and December 1962). Papers from other seminars in the series have been published as *The Teaching of Architecture* (Washington: The American Institute of Architects, 1964) and *The History, Theory and Criticism of Architecture* (Cambridge: The M. I. T. Press, 1965).

Marcus Whiffen

Arizona State University
May 1966

Contents

The Architect and the City

His Role and Training Yesterday, Today, and Tomorrow

G. HOLMES PERKINS

We are prone to confuse the roles of architect and city planner. In a conference such as this, there are always those who would (unless we mistake their meaning) graft onto the architect the highly developed analytical skills of the economist and sociologist. I would suggest to you, however, that the essence of the architect's contribution to the city and to society is now, and should always be, the sincere and undivided dedication to creative design. His ability to invest each structure and space with qualities that stimulate new and unforeseen responses places upon him a double burden, for he must in a single act serve the present while opening the door to tomorrow. His is the decisive role in creating tomorrow's urban environment. I say this knowing very well that there are many forces that are beyond his control.

There are many things about which he does not know enough ever to compete with the experts. There are economic decisions to be made from which he, perhaps too often, is excluded; there are political decisions that frustrate him and make his life intolerable; and there are technological developments over which he has little control. In spite of these things, I say that his will be the decisive role. In spite of his lack of knowledge of the social sciences and the present deplorable state of his education, he will still be the leader.

Under these circumstances, it is hardly surprising that our architectural visions have been so limited that we have had to depend heavily upon intuition. It is not surprising that we have failed to reflect in our designs the potential richness of urban social life and have relied too much on norms and averages for guidance, rather than on a true and human understanding of the individual.

Taking, on the other hand, the long view of the architect's role, one can see a steady widening of the architect's social responsibilities and an expansion of his technical competence. There are few of us here today who were trained in the classical orders as the basis for architectural design. Since those days the ideas of Morris, of Wright, and of the Bauhaus have entered the picture and are already as much a part of our rich architectural heritage of theory as the earlier theories of Alberti, Palladio, and Guadet.

Today the architect, like the scientist, is plagued by the sudden expansion of knowledge. Robert Oppenheimer, speaking at the AIA convention in San Francisco in 1959, said that of the major discoveries in science since the beginning of recorded history, more than nine out of ten were made by men living today. Perhaps in architecture we have not advanced quite so rapidly; but still the atmosphere and character of our profession is utterly different from what it was two or three decades ago.

The architect of tomorrow will operate almost entirely in an urban setting. The major urban areas of the United States will probably grow by ninety million persons in the next twenty years. This growth will be accompanied by an absolute decline in the rural population. The overwhelming physical impact upon the city will be accompanied by the frightening problem of social adjustment as people move from the farm and smaller communities to the metropolis.

The architect of tomorrow will operate in a highly competitive society where within the urban areas there is already a marked exodus of the well-to-do from the central parts of the cities to the suburbs. There is also a return migration into the centers by some of these people; but the majority are moving away from the center. If the vacated areas could be redeveloped at new and higher standards, this movement pattern might be a blessing in disguise. But here you are running hard against the social problems raised by segregation — the segregation of the less well-to-do who remain within the city core from those who can afford to escape. In other words, the well-to-do whose family backgrounds have given them a sound tradition and a sense of self-control and social responsibility have moved to the suburbs. There, where perhaps education for the children is least needed, education is at its best. The school budget per pupil within the central areas of our cities today, in areas where you have the greatest need for good education, runs to approximately $300 per pupil per year. In contrast, in the suburbs, where family backgrounds are so much better and the opportunities so much greater, the expenditure per pupil runs $800–900 per year. This maladjustment is but one of many that will have an enormous impact upon the architecture of our urban complexes.

Tomorrow's architect will be operating in a state of constant and accelerating change. He will be operating in a surplus economy whose productive capacity is no longer a limiting factor in choice. In other words, we can no longer excuse ourselves for doing the second-rate thing because we could not afford the best.

Let us take the case of urban renewal. Today this is one of the largest businesses in the nation. I do not know the figures in other cities, but in Philadelphia the Planning Commission recently allocated over $200,000,000 for clearance of land alone in the next six years, without counting the cost of any rebuilding. Now this may be rather high compared with other cities, but it is not enough.

The purpose of urban renewal was, first of all, if you go back to the 1949 Act, to provide safe and sanitary housing. This is all very well; no one will object. That notion, however, has been expanded in the successive amendments and in the administrative interpretations of the law, until now the cities use their urban renewal powers for the preservation and the creation of a sound tax base. A sound tax base is necessary if we are to provide the public services that every city needs. Neither can you object to this. Furthermore, it is used to create jobs, to prevent industry from escaping to the suburbs, or to steal industry from somebody else and to make it come to your city rather than to some other. These are all laudable objectives. They are objectives we can all applaud. But I shall suggest to you that there is much to be said for Huxley's view:

> At present our approach is concerned almost entirely with economics, social security and physical health. This material approach is frankly not enough. However adequately it deals with the foundations of life, it leaves out all its upper stories. Our new view of human destiny insists that emotional, intellectual and spiritual satisfactions must also be taken into account.

In recent times there has been a tendency to recognize Huxley's admonition to us. In recent renewal programs there have been provisions for educational institutions, for recreation, for many of the amenities that are needed in the city, and money is being spent on these. But what is more significant than that, in several recent urban renewal competitions of importance the decisions have not been based on financing or economics or densities. These competitions have been decided upon the basis of architecture interpreted in the largest sense, in the sense that this design is capable beyond all other designs of creating a humane environment for urban living. Each one of these has been won on that basis, the best that could be achieved at that time. We should not remain satisfied with that — I am not sure that they are the best of all possible designs — but this is the basis upon which they were judged, and this is significant.

You do not need greater productivity to produce a humane

environment; in fact, in none of these cities, I would say, do you have a humane environment that compares with that of Venice, built in a time of low productivity, but where standards were set and decisions were made that became lasting ones, which we still can admire hundreds of years later. Our heritage from Venice can never be measured in dollars.

I should like to suggest that we have a long way to go before we shall be able to cope with certain very difficult problems. Our educational facilities are way behind the times. Let us compare for a moment our own present state of affairs with that of the medical profession. The medical profession sixty years ago met the challenge with which we are faced today. I am not suggesting that there is any close analogy between medical and architectural education, but there are still many basic lessons to be learned. In the first quarter of this century, Sir William Osler, helped by Carnegie and Rockefeller grants, set up a new form of medical education. The doctors recognized that scientific medicine became the objective, specialization the dominant pattern, and the university medical center the preferred instrument. In about 1925 the idea of scientific medicine began to be modified by a new outlook in education: the concept of comprehensive medicine with its interest in the whole man, in his emotional well-being, in his home, and in his community environment.

Are we not entering just such a phase in architecture? Are we not equally committed to a concern with man's total physical environment? As the architects of cities and regions, we must accept full responsibility, and we must educate our successors in such a way that they can create a humane and delightful environment in harmony with nature. I suggest that such widened and deepened responsibilities will force a lengthening of our present architectural curricula and re-emphasize the advantages of a sounder liberal education.

In medicine this need was recognized early in the century. In 1904 only four out of the 160 medical schools required any college work before admission. By 1918, only fourteen years later, this was mandatory in eighty-five out of ninety-five schools.

By 1954, three quarters of all medical students had completed four years of liberal arts before starting their professional courses. What is even more important, by that time the schools had discovered how to pick their students. We have not learned this. In 1954 in the first-year class in the medical schools, the drop-out rate was reduced to less than 5 per cent. Now, this is in shocking contrast to the human and financial waste that characterizes undergraduate architectural education in the United States. Those of you who have read the report of the Educational Testing Service will recognize that of the twelve schools tested over the past five years, only a quarter to a third of the students are likely to graduate with their class. In fact, in one school that had an entering freshman class of 115, only one man graduated on schedule.

This problem is, of course, further compounded by the necessity to expand the services rendered by the architect. The AIA, through its Committee on the Profession, has recognized this. As yet, action is not definite, but we are beginning to consider these problems. The AIA and the ACSA have created a three-man commission to look at the educational problems growing out of these expanded services, which will inevitably force specialization upon us no matter how the AIA votes in the Convention against recognition of this trend. It is upon us and will become more pronounced as time goes by.

This specialization will require some re-examination of our concept of the architect. It will require a lengthening of his period of training and a broadening of his liberal education. It will require us to recognize that if we are to be a profession, there must be significant research backed by individuals, the profession, and the schools. This does not mean that as architects we are to abandon architecture to become research people. There will be very few of us who have either the talent or the interest in these areas. I place engineering among them, as well as economics and sociology. We shall have to hire people competent in these fields, just as the doctors brought in the biologist to do much of the basic research as a part of the team until he was employed in the hospital and in the medical schools. He is not an outsider; he is part of the profession, and he is recognized as such. He makes his livelihood and his reputation within this new field, and so I believe we must recognize our fellows who will do corresponding work for us in the future.

Now urban design is perhaps the primary responsibility of the architect. His interest and his acts will impinge upon the landscape, on art, on city planning, on engineering — in fact, upon the total urban environment. Yet his training is quite inadequate. Let me repeat again, however, that it is my belief that the essence of the architect's professional contribution to society is, and should remain, his unique dedication to creative design.

In order to make this contribution, we must obtain the same stature as a profession as some of our fellow professions now have. I believe that the basic necessity is a firmer and a longer liberal education. I include in this liberal education both drawing and basic design, for I believe that these are as important a language as the spoken or the written word, and not only should this language be available to those in the profession, but it should be an essential ingredient of the education of everyone. A number of years ago, President Lowell of Harvard spoke of a liberal education as the best of all preparations for meeting those countless situations where sound decisions based upon inadequate evidence are required.

Four uncommitted years offer the student an unrivaled opportunity to develop a sound judgment as to the choice of his future career. Our present system, which often forces premature decisions, is the root of much tragic waste and mounting frustration. For many trapped students there is no honorable escape. A liberal arts course of not less than two years, and preferably of four, would foster maturity and judgment, and at the same time would provide a built-in escape hatch for those who have found other interests. Most important of all, it would improve the public image of the architect. It is well to remember that our fellow professionals in law and medicine are characteristically products of graduate schools. The same trend is very clear in that brash newcomer among the professions, business education. These are the men with whom we shall have to deal in our professional careers, and I believe the architect deserves and needs an education no less rigorous and broad.

In trying to identify the guidelines for decisions, we should examine just what they ought to be rather than what they are at present. In a democratic society, I believe that the days of economic determinism are past; that the day of technocracy is over. This is not to deny that technology is one of the determinants of form, whether it be in the single building or in the city. But, by itself, it is not adequate; "It leaves out all those spiritual and intellectual elements," as Huxley tells us.

Therefore, in terms of tomorrow's guidelines, I suggest that we judge the value of a design on the basis of its ability to promote social values and to provide variety and freedom of choice that will include contrast, a hierarchy of spaces, and an infinite variety of opportunities; that we favor the design that will most effectively encourage constant renewal and healthy growth; and that we recognize man and all his works as a part of nature.

If the architect were to prepare himself adequately to participate in decision making upon the basis of such criteria, he must obviously have some understanding, though not expert knowledge, in many areas. As a citizen and layman, he should concern himself with this decision-making process. Well-informed, active, and public-minded groups can have an enormous influence on the decision-making process. Yet the architect, as an architect, must at the same time have the vision to stir men's hearts and to produce designs upon which others less professionally competent can base a decision. He must participate in the programming and budgeting process. I know that it bores most architects, but it is at the program stage that many of the decisions that we later complain about are made. It is at this stage that densities are decided and that the principles and policies establishing segregation are involved. I am not talking about racial segregation only. We have all kinds of segregation — of business properties from residential properties, of single-family houses from multiple-family houses, etc. As an example, I can point to a magnificent design for a new subdivision for four hundred homes that was submitted to the Philadelphia Planning Commission recently. Since, to our mind, it was one of the best proposals we had ever seen, we were prepared to approve it even though it included row houses for an area zoned for single-family houses. The design left much open space, preserved the trees, and respected the topography. However, there was a violent and nearly unanimous outcry from four hundred neighbors because it would upset the pattern of their single-family neighborhood. They had been sold the notion that this kind of segregation had some social value and that this preserved financial investment. In fact, this kind of segregation is just as dangerous as racial segregation.

It is at the program and policy-making level that these decisions are made, and not on the drawing board. Then it is too late. You have to know enough about these other problems so that you can prevent mistakes; you must know the consequences of the decision that some lawyer in the Planning Commission or the Redevelopment Authority may not know. He may for very honest and very real reasons say that this is the right solution. But he may not know the consequences of his act. You must understand the design repercussions of the economic, political, or social decisions that are proposed, and you must be able to advise as the expert in this area.

It is demanding to be such an expert, for the instruments with which we have to work are changing. The scale of development is enormous. Before the war about nine tenths of our housing was erected by operators who built less than ten houses a year. Today almost the reverse is the case. The big operator is in the saddle. This is true for urban redevelopment, business properties, housing, institutions, and so on. Not only is the scale larger, but the methods of financing have changed to make this possible. The technology of building and the nature of the contractor have changed. Governmental participation has become vital to the success of almost every project. You must understand the role of each of the people involved. You cannot be the financier, you cannot be the realtor, you cannot be the government bureaucrat, you cannot be all of these people, although individuals may participate in each one of these areas. But you must understand the reasons why these experts act as they do, and you must be able to guide them and show them still better ways of working so that we shall have a more humane city tomorrow.

We must be far more cognizant of the role of history in the making of cities, and have an understanding of time as one of the basic design elements. Architectural history as given in most [illegible] today avoids any talk of the city. Our students [illegible] the dates of the cathedrals and the palaces, but their relationship to urban design is one of the neglected elements in our curricula today. To my mind, it is far more important to understand the history of our cities and their ways of growth than the evolution of architectural styles.

In building tomorrow's cities, we are not going to be able to wipe the slate clean and build monuments to ourselves or to our generation, though this has been for all men a terrible temptation. Instead, we must search for new answers. Organized research must be vigorously fostered by the schools and the profession; an atmosphere of exploration and experimentation must pervade the school.

There are two research paths open to us. One is the path of experience and practice. It offers some rich opportunities to test ideas, although the room for experimentation is severely limited by most clients. The second path is organized research within a school under the leadership of experiment-minded teachers. Of these there are far too few, and there are even fewer who understand the methods of research, which is a special skill all its own. And yet, to my mind, an active program of research is indispensable to the promotion of an atmosphere of learning whose prime purpose is the discovery of natural laws, of human reactions to space, color, form, and technical innovation, and the creation of a more humane environment. To those of you who may one day have to tangle with budgets, I suggest that budgeting is a tool that will allow you to enrich the quality and depth of your faculty by dividing salaries between two budgets — one for architecture and one for planning. Our own experience in city planning has shown beyond question the value of such a budgetary device, for only by this method have we been able to hold such an unusually talented and varied faculty.

The essence of a school is obviously the attitude and quality of its faculty. Particularly in this day and age when specialization is forced upon us, we must exert a special effort to preserve the unity of the design professions. Under the umbrella of a single faculty dedicated to the design of the total environment, there should be programs in landscape, in structural and mechanical engineering, in art, in planning, and in architecture. Each one will contribute its share to the common cause. Because of the fragmentation of the professions that prevails today, good candidates are often not attracted to some of the areas with which we are deeply concerned. This is particularly notable in engineering, where the more talented are seduced by the glamour and the high rewards of rocketry and electronics. We are just not getting enough good men in the vital but less exciting areas. The engineers recognize this problem, and they are as concerned as we are in architecture. I believe that the only solution is the creation of a new faculty with the emphasis on creativity, which can bring a heightened prestige to all of the design professions.

In designing the new curricula, we must pay more attention to the forces that mold our cities and our architecture. Systems of pedestrian and vehicular movement evoke new forms. The decisions of government design our buildings for us; investment policies and even myths affect our work. If we wish to be masters in our own house, we must learn to manipulate these forces as well as we now integrate our spaces and our structural systems. Such curricula would roughly correspond to the basic medical and clinical studies of the doctor, but we have no comparable internship. The hospital offers the doctor firm assurance of the continuation of his education with increasing responsibilities. Industry offers similar openings to the engineer. The present structure of our profession offers no continuation, nor does it offer any real assurance of an organized sequence of practical experience. Action to fill this void is the joint responsibility of the profession and the schools. I see no other way for us. At the present stage of development of our profession, we architects cannot provide the internship unaided. It must be a joint responsibility; and the schools, I think, will have to take the lead and share the cost. I know I impose upon the schools an almost impossible burden, and I do not expect that anybody is likely to follow this road tomorrow. I hope, however, that in the great variety of schools across the country, many experiments will be tried, that we shall learn from each other's successes and shortcomings, and that over a period of ten years or even a generation we shall solve our problems as the doctors have solved many of their problems in the thirty years that have just gone by.

Let me say in closing that in spite of all this discussion of a new vision and a new concept of the architect, at bottom the architect is the architect of old. It is the same old challenge, and our response to this challenge, I believe, is most eloquently described by Le Corbusier when he says:

> The architect by his arrangement of forms realizes an order which is a pure creation of his spirit. By forms he affects our senses to an acute degree and provokes plastic emotions; by the relationships which he creates, he awakens profound echoes in us, he gives the measure of an order which we feel to be in accordance with that of our world, he determines the various movements of our heart and of our understanding; it is then that we experience the sense of beauty.*

*_Towards a New Architecture_, translated by Frederick Etchells (London: The Architectural Press, 1926), p. 7.

The Purpose of the City

Changing City Landscapes as Manifestations of Cultural Values

JOHN B. JACKSON

Three separate city landscapes, three urban environments: these are what I should like to explore with you, not as architects or as city planners, but simply as persons interested in their surroundings and in trying to understand them. The three that I have chosen have commonplace names: the Baroque, the Romantic, and the Contemporary. I realize that these terms are far from precise; they are convenient, however, for distinguishing three periods in our Western culture.

By contrasting these city landscapes, by noting what each of them has borrowed or rejected, it is possible, I think, to approach some understanding of the urban landscape that is evolving around us, and the role that every urban landscape plays in our lives. For each city landscape, and indeed each human landscape, urban or rural, represents a unique way of organizing space and activity in order to achieve a desirable purpose. If you ask me what that purpose is, I shall beg the question by saying that it varies from one period to another.

The Baroque City Landscape

It is customary, I believe, to define the Baroque Age as the years between 1600 and 1750 — give or take a decade or two at either end. I have no quarrel with that definition, except that I like to think that we can look upon an age not simply as an interval between events but as an event in its own right. In that sense the Baroque Age is the rebirth of Rome, the city, much as the age that followed it, the Romantic, is the growth of Paris and London.

By the middle of the sixteenth century, Rome was fast coming to life after generations of neglect and decay. The new Cathedral of St. Peter was at last being built. The Popes took pains to beautify and enlarge the city, and in the older quarters as on the surrounding hills splendid palaces, churches, villas, and monuments were rising. Noble families came to live in Rome, to play a role in politics, or to spend their wealth. In their wake came countless artists and architects, painters and sculptors, actors and writers and musicians, and a horde of tourists, adventurers, and students. By the end of the century the population had tripled to become 100,000, the appearance of the city was largely changed, and everyone in Europe who wanted to acquire polish, and at the same time enjoy himself, found his way to Rome during the winter season, even though it meant a tiresome journey of several weeks by coach or horseback through dangerous country. In the Papal possessions alone there were supposed to be no less than 16,000 bandits.

Once arrived, the tourist divided his time between culture and entertainment. There were the classical ruins to see, though they were fast being torn down in the course of the Baroque urban renewal; there were inscriptions to read and dutifully copy, galleries and collections to visit. And once these things had been done, there were parties, balls, theaters, games, and above all the Roman carnival to enjoy.

But probably the most entertaining aspect of Rome was Rome itself, the never-ending variety of the life in the streets and squares and courtyards. From early in the morning until dark the city resounded with a bewildering assortment of activities, engaged in by people of every class and age and origin: vendors of fruit and cold drinks and sausages, marionette players, beggars, fashionable sightseers, and constant processions of priests, soldiers, visiting celebrities, weddings, funerals, and ever and anon the carriages and sedan chairs of the rich. "Most people in Rome," a French traveler observed in the seventeenth century, "do absolutely nothing. A true Roman gets up early and goes strolling until the heat of the day begins, then he takes a nap and stays in bed until afternoon. At sundown he goes strolling, comes home for supper, and goes out in the evening, lantern in hand, for pleasure." The dark and narrow streets, without any public lighting whatsoever — that was a late eighteenth-century innovation — were ideal places for adventures of every kind.

An important part of this animated public life was the large official procession. A typical event was the arrival in the mid-seventeenth century of the son of the king of Poland who came as his father's ambassador. He passed in triumph through the city, accompanied by 160 carriages. The next day he made his ceremonial appearance in a carefully staged parade to the Vatican, where he paid his respects to the Pope. There were trumpeters with silver trumpets, musicians, ten camels with ostrich plumes and silver bells, thirty-four Cossack riders with bows and arrows, thirty pages in blue satin on matched sorrel horses. (By a well-calculated mishap one of the horses lost a shoe; it was of the finest gold, and the population of Rome remembered the episode for decades.) Finally the Polish prince himself appeared, covered with diamonds and sables on a resplendent horse; and as the parade approached the Vatican, cannon sounded a salute. In the evening there were gala performances in a public square and an elaborate display of fireworks.

Even the smaller processions were spectacular, and at any hour of the day a cardinal might pass through the city in his sedan chair, and everyone would stop what he was doing and kneel in the street. Outside the churches trumpeters and drummers proclaimed special religious services with newly composed music. In many public squares on the right day or season you could buy anything from fresh vegetables, or sherbet made from snow brought from the mountains, to antique coins and herbs for any ailment. John Evelyn, the celebrated English diarist who came to Rome for the carnival of 1645 (and who incidentally wrote one of the very first treatises against air pollution, *Fumifugium*, in which he recommended that trees be planted in London to purify the air), described the extraordinary scene: wild races of riderless horses down one of the important streets of the city, and itinerant theaters, mounted on the back of oxcarts. "The streets," he remarked, "are swarming with whores, buffoons, and all manner of rabble." Pageantry of this sort must have been fascinating to watch, at least for a few days; perhaps it is even more fascinating to read about. The reason I mention it, however, is that it suggests two very significant characteristics of the Baroque city landscape.

The first of these characteristics is an obvious one, but one we are inclined to forget: a rich and varied street life, like that of Rome or any other European city of the period, means that there is no other place for many of these activities. The Baroque city did not provide its citizens with small private or specialized areas. All but the very rich lived in crowded and promiscuous quarters, and even the rich lacked the secluded living rooms, patios, and studies that most of our homes possess. Sir Henry Wotton, in his *Elements of Architecture*, wrote: "I observe no nation in the world by nature more private and reserved than the Italian, and on the other side in no habitations less privacy; so as there is a conflict between their dwelling and their being."

When a Roman of the Baroque Age wanted to converse with friends or sought a degree of privacy, the street was the best place to go; and when he had business to transact, he again went into the street or square. We are, in fact, very familiar with this practice from the plays of Shakespeare, in which a public square is very often the scene of the most intimate conversation.

It is well to remember that to have street after street devoted exclusively to business, as in the modern city, is something relatively new. It is part of our modern tendency to develop specialized areas in the city. Two hundred years ago and more, retail merchants displayed their wares in temporary stands or in the public square. Our two words "shop" and "store" hark back to that arrangement; a shop was a place where an artisan worked (as in "machine shop"), a store a place where the merchant stored his wares. It was, in fact, the custom of open-air selling that helped make the Baroque city so lively a place.

What is likely to astonish us most about the Baroque city landscape is the number of activities that were outdoor and public two centuries ago but that have in the meantime withdrawn from public view. Almost all retail business is, of course, now transacted in its own specialized areas, just as manufacturing is. Social intercourse has to a large extent gone into seclusion in homes, clubs, bars, and restaurants. The theater (or its popular equivalent, the movie) now has its own special precinct, and the church festival is more often than not a subdued affair in the basement. The pageantry of visiting dignitaries has become a dull and graceless spectacle: a brief glimpse of a motorcycle escort, a half-dozen black limousines, and a few flags. All that we have retained of the Baroque street pageantry is the circus parade and the funeral.

But if the Baroque city lacked the private specialized areas that we have since developed in such numbers, it had a great many public areas. The most familiar example is the piazza, or public square; thus, if I were to choose the typical space form for that period, I should choose the square, just as I should choose the park for the Romantic period, and the highway for the Contemporary period. But in addition to the Baroque public square, there were also the courtyard of the house, the formal rooms of the house itself, the garden, and even the church. I doubt if many of us would consider any of these last places as public. We think of the house, the individual room, the garden, and the church as private to the point of sanctity. Yet Alberti, who, though he wrote in the fifteenth century, was much admired in the Baroque Age, compared the courtyard of the house to a public square, for it was there that strangers as well as friends forgathered, where food was bought and sold, and where many of the household chores were done with everyone looking on. Evelyn commented on the enormous number of what he called "common rooms" — meaning public rooms — in the palaces of Rome, and we are all familiar with the strange ceremonies of Louis XIV, whose dressing and undressing and going to bed were witnessed not only by those noblemen lucky enough to hold his stockings or his wig but by a sizable crowd of spectators who paid for the privilege. I suppose we are all equally familiar with those Baroque engravings of church interiors showing groups of men, hats on, swords at their hips, chatting with friends. In the Jesuit church in Rome, hot chocolate was served during Mass, and bunches of flowers were distributed to the ladies.

To me it is striking that the garden, which we consider a private domain, was in the Baroque city a public domain. In most European cities of the period only the well-to-do could afford gardens, and parks and promenades and tree-lined avenues were very rare indeed. Nevertheless, it seems to have been a point of honor with most of the rich to let the public come into their gardens whenever they wanted to, although it is true some owners posted fierce penalties for anyone who occupied their favorite bench. A Baroque book on garden design specifies that the paths be broad for dancing, and that summer houses and pavilions be used for musicians or for serving refreshments. The garden was altogether a very sociable place, and it would be a serious mistake on our part to think of the Baroque garden in modern terms. It was not meant for solitude; it was meant for people.

But there is another characteristic that ought not to be overlooked and that again distinguishes the Baroque city landscape from our own. The street scene in Rome and elsewhere constantly reminded the citizen that he lived in a strictly ordered, hierarchical society, a society organized according to rank, class, grade, or birth. Much of the Baroque landscape was designed to dramatize this principle. The Baroque parade, like the Baroque spectacle, should in a sense be understood in this light — as a visible demonstration of social purpose and order; the succession of participants, building up to a climax, was a matter not only of art but of social hierarchy. A Pope's birthday celebration, the funeral of a cardinal, the anniversary of a saint, an important wedding or funeral — these were very intricate organizations of precedence and rank. In 1584, a hospital for crippled beggars was opened in Rome with an elaborate parade — arranged, of course, in a hierarchical order: first a chorus and a band by way of overture, then a troop of able-bodied beggars, then fourteen wagonloads of the bedridden, then the priests in charge. This grisly procession wound through the busiest streets of Rome demonstrating among other things that charity had its ranks and orders. In Vienna the Baroque passion for parades reached such a pitch that they were staged for no good reason at all. Everyone at the court appeared in classical costume, special music was composed, and the whole affair ended with the customary display of fireworks — arranged of course in dramatic order. The only modern instance that I can think of resembling this Baroque heritage is a formal church wedding where the guests are seated according to a kind of rank, and where there is a short procession of bridesmaids and then the bride. And it was not only in public parades that the Baroque spirit showed this liking for hierarchy: Spanish etiquette, which was extraordinarily stiff and elaborate, transformed the domestic life of the rich in their palaces into lengthy ceremonies, well worth watching, showing rank and precedence. Church services were almost operatic in their elaborate ritualized splendor, and even the day-by-day life of the city suggested a permanent, almost cosmic order: on certain days of the week certain markets were held, certain days were holidays, certain seasons brought with them other activities, duly acknowledged by a procession or a service. Even the times of day had their appropriate end and beginning. Wherever the citizen looked, wherever he went, he was reminded of a permanent order behind an apparent confusion.

But to repeat, inherent in all these schemes was a feeling for caste or class. The princes and those with titles automatically occupied the best position in every spatial design, whether in the procession, in the church service, or in the layout of the city. Next came the middle class. The ground floor in most palaces was thus reserved for artisans and small merchants; to this day the street floor of many Italian palaces contains shops and booths and tenements. Even in the Louvre in Paris there were

society of buildings," and perhaps it is the appearance or the design of the buildings that indicates their social standing rather than their location or function.

I have said all about the Baroque city landscape that I need to say for my present purpose. The subject may seem remote and of little current interest, but I am convinced that the truth is otherwise. The fact is that most of us have at one time or another come in close contact with a Baroque environment, and many of us have an instinctive liking for it. There are evidences of it, of course, in the Roman Catholic Church, with its complicated hierarchy, its ritual, its humanism. And most of us, I suspect, have met the Baroque environment in a less attractive but no less genuine form — in the United States Army. There we find the same enthusiasm for parades and formations, the same lack of any feeling for privacy, the same fanatic addiction to privilege and rank — indeed, the same weakness for fireworks, particularly rockets. There is even a kind of inverted humanism in the military exploitation of nature entirely for the purpose of destroying man. And I need not point out the Baroque way in which the Army approaches the whole question of function versus status: the first is a temporary attribute, haphazardly bestowed, while the latter is permanent and essential.

Many traits of the Baroque Age seem to be coming back to life, and many are being deliberately fostered. I happen to admire a great deal about the Baroque point of view; I like its formality, its vigor, its humanism; I even have a certain sympathy for a sound order that recognizes differences and puts them to use instead of pretending they do not exist. But I think we should take a second look at its shortcomings, insofar as they might have bearing on the landscape of the future. First, the emphasis on a hierarchical rather than a functional organization of society is hostile to any easy growth or change. That is obvious. The second trait is one I find much more dangerous precisely because its seems to have a growing appeal. I refer to the disregard for private life, for the individual inner experience. The Baroque Age had little or no understanding of the importance of interior existence, speaking psychologically as well as architecturally, with the result that the age that came after it — the age that started before the French Revolution and lasted until about the Second World War — went to the other extreme, and emphasized the individual experience, the individual environment, at the expense of the whole city landscape.

The Romantic City Landscape

When we read the history of the eighteenth century with the city landscape in mind, we are likely to be surprised by the number of hints of a change in store for the Baroque city; they cluster around the year 1750, it seems to me, but some of them are earlier and some of them later. Let me give a few. In 1760 the French architect Patte wrote: "Hitherto we have sacrificed too much to magnificence, but we have never tried to insure a fine well-being to men, to preserve their lives, their health, and to assure the wholesomeness of the air in their dwellings." In 1738 Louis XV decided to move out of Versailles Palace into a smaller, more intimate residence. In 1728 — very early, really — a book appeared in Paris with the first collection of architectural designs for small middle-class dwellings. In 1742 the first book on Gothic architecture appeared, in which it was declared that "the best Gothic buildings in magnificence and beauty greatly exceed all that have been done by both Greeks and moderns." In 1748 one of the very first zoning ordinances was passed: the city of Aix-en-Provence forbade any booths or stands on the central promenade of the city, which was to be reserved for pedestrians and cafés. In 1755 the French architectural critic Laugier remarked: "We must look at the city as a forest. The streets of the city are the roads of the forest, and should be cut through in the same manner."

All of these instances come from France, but there are easily as many from Germany and England. Indeed the most significant of all from my point of view comes from England, for it was in that country that the first informal landscape gardens were designed in the 1730's or 1740's (according to one's definition of informality in this context).

I would not say that all of these dates are important in the wider context of history; but each of them marks a change, or the promise of a change, in the urban environment. What inspired them is something else again. We are familiar with the usual textbook explanations: the beginnings of democracy, the rise of capitalism, the dawn of the industrial revolution, the introduction of sentiment and emotion into art, the rediscovery of nature, and so on. I am certainly not equipped to dispute these explanations. But I feel that beneath all these changes was a change in the way men defined themselves, the new identity that they assumed in their own eyes, their gradual awareness of their own importance. They were disenchanted with their identity as social beings (which was their Baroque identity) and began to see themselves as more or less unique individuals, each of them privileged or, if you prefer, obliged to make his own adjustment to the surrounding world.

In any event, the explanation for this change in attitude toward the landscape is not our business; we are concerned with how this change affected the city. And to put it simply and crudely, what happened was that people lost interest in traditional man-made public areas, and they started, very tentatively at first, to design and create a whole series of small specialized areas, unique environments, small individual worlds for one specific purpose only. This is how I interpret the new feeling in the mid-eighteenth century for domestic life, for the home as an environment for bringing up children, as a private world to be made comfortable and secluded and detached from the workaday outside world. And this is also how I interpret the new feeling for informal gardens as areas for the private experience of nature. So much has been written about the romantic aesthetic sentiment for nature that I hesitate to add more than a few words; to me it represents less a love of nature than a distaste for society.

The most obvious instance of an urge to create and control a small private environment is the rise of the suburb with its detached, freestanding house. Country residences near the city have always existed, of course, but the suburb, as I understand it, represents among other things a complete elimination of rural as well as urban social ties: the suburbanite does not farm or have a cow; at most he has an ornamental garden. Again it was in the middle of the eighteenth century that this became a noticeable movement; and Paris was among the first cities where it occurred. Hitherto that city had been typically Baroque, if not in the architecture at least in its self-containment. Its amusements had been group amusements, and its contacts with nature had been what we would now call artificial. In one of his satires Boileau very minutely describes the confusion and variety of seventeenth-century Paris life. Then, with comparative suddenness, the well-to-do middle class and the aristocracy decided to desert their palaces and mansions in the crowded downtown section. For generations they and their ancestors had lived cheek by jowl with tenements, taverns, workshops, stables, lodging houses, without ever finding the relationship objectionable. But after that fateful decade in the mid-eighteenth century they began to build houses in the new western section where the Etoile and the Champs Elysées and the Parc Monceau are now located. Real estate operators and speculators had much to do with the boom. The brothers of Louis XVI made a great deal of money subdividing their property, and Balzac's novels describe how fortunes were made and lost in the building frenzy after the Revolution.

As a result of the migration of wealth and taste, the older part of Paris soon became the slum that much of it still is; the newer part, which is still the fashionable section of Paris, was more open, with wider streets, quieter and more private. A new and more isolated way of living became possible for the rich inhabitants of this western district.

The usual explanation for the development of the suburb is the much-discussed rediscovery of nature. But Lewis Mumford, for instance, does not mention it. What he does say is that the flight from the city was inspired by a desire

> to be your own unique self, to build your unique home, and a unique landscape. To live a self-centered life in which private fantasy and caprice would have license to express themselves openly; in short, to withdraw like a monk and live like a prince.

Philippe Aries, writing in a recent issue of *Landscape* on the growth of Paris, ascribes the migration to much the same causes — to a desire for privacy and isolation. And if I may be allowed to add a comment, I would say that back of the movement was not only a desire for privacy but a desire to eliminate workaday concerns from the private environment. To be specific, people wished to separate as far as possible the place of work from the place of residence.

Thus the logical result of the migration to the suburbs was a division of the city, at least for the well-to-do, into two distinct parts, a residential part and a work or business part; when railroads and large industrial installations came to Paris, the working class experienced the same division between residence and place of work. As we all know, these divisions in the city multiplied in the course of the nineteenth century. It would be far-fetched to ascribe them to psychological factors alone; there were economic and topographical factors also at work. But I think a very important urge in the nineteenth century was to remove the place of dwelling from any risk of contamination by society; if we now have sections of the city exclusively devoted to amusement, education, finance, retail, wholesale activities, etc., it is largely because the family moved out of them into a more congenial residential area. And it is interesting to note that one of the earliest ideal industrial cities, the town of Chaux, designed by Nicolas Ledoux in the 1780's and 1790's, incorporates these specialized areas as evidently very desirable. There is, first of all, a distinct separation between dwelling and place of work, an emphasis on streets and avenues instead of public squares (because communication between the various districts was more important than places for public gathering), and an extraordinary proliferation of buildings with specialized functions, including a Paciferium (for making up quarrels), a temple of memory to the Glory of Women, and a House of Honor consecrated to the cult of moral values. Ledoux's plan illustrates another conspicuous feature of the Romantic city landscape: the public building or monument isolated in the midst of its own individual space or environment. The American county courthouse, standing by itself in a square, is merely a small-town counterpart of the freestanding museum or school or public library or state capitol to be found in countless nineteenth-century cities. Sigfried Giedion's first published book, incidentally, dealt largely with this matter of individualistic isolation in architecture. Whatever its inspiration, it marked the end, I think, of that humanist simile that saw the city as a society of buildings.

The manner in which the growth of individualism, of self-awareness, affected the Romantic city landscape is known to us all; the detached houses, the variegated architecture, the many different functional areas of the nineteenth-century city are all evidence of it. But when I mention a second characteristic of the Romantic city, its cult of nature, I think some explanation is due. The cult had two distinct aspects. Obviously, we have the aesthetic cult of nature to thank for our parks and public gardens, for the introduction of greenery into our cities, for the insistence on fresh air and sunlight and contact with the unspoiled landscape. We can also thank that phase of the cult for much of our finest painting and poetry and music; in short, we can thank the cult for many of the things we value most highly in our contemporary civilization. But the cult of nature had another, less fortunate aspect; it induced us to turn to nature and what was supposed to be the law of nature for guidance in ethical and social matters. Thus it was that the Romantic Age discovered that society (and in particular the nation and the city) was no longer to be understood in outworn humanistic terms — to say nothing of theological terms — but in terms of the laws and processes of nature. The nation and the city were looked upon as spontaneous forms of life, organisms that men were to respect and admire but not seek to control. Men did not have the right or the power to interfere in natural processes; men did not have the right to establish goals or to set limits to the expansion of these organisms, for nature was working toward its own inscrutable ends. They might at most prune and chip a little here and there, or encourage the organism to grow in one direction more than the other. But just as we do not usually say to a plant "develop into such and such a form, and then stop growing," we cannot (so the Romantic citizen thought) say of a city or a nation that it had now reached the right size, that it was time for it to assume its final form. Perhaps this is the significance of the remark I cited earlier that compared the city to a forest; it showed that at a very early date people had begun to think of the city as being a law unto itself, a kind of wilderness that produced its own beauty and achieved its own health and balance without the intercession of ignorant man. It is important to note that the only criterion nature seemed to provide for the well-being of an organism was appetite and size. The bigger, the faster-growing, the more voracious the organisms, the better.

We all have reason to be familiar with the political implications of this biological fallacy; the notion of *Lebensraum*, of living space for a society, a mid-nineteenth-century invention, has cost us two wars and fostered nineteenth-century nationalism and imperialism. And it is significant that *Lebensraum* means, not the space a people *at present* occupies, but the space it would need when it inevitably expands. This it seems to me is the dream of the private or exclusive environment carried to its nightmare conclusion. But the nineteenth-century city also had to have its *Lebensraum*; it also had to devour its weaker and smaller neighbors. And it was also the law of nature that within the city, as within the jungle, only the fittest survived or flourished. The past was swept out of the way. The nineteenth-century city was thus a landscape to be explored and exploited — and how many Victorian novels there are that tell of the young man coming to the big city to make his fortune, to conquer all obstacles and bring home a prize! He does not go to the city to become civilized; he does not go as one would go to join a distinguished society of educated men; he goes there to exploit its riches, and to heighten his own individuality.

I do not mean to imply that the inhabitants of the Romantic city were always enthusiastic about the lawless landscape they inhabited; we all know how eloquent were the critics of the city, particularly in the latter half of the nineteenth century.

But the average city dweller, and probably the average office-holder as well, was spiritually hamstrung by this belief in the supremacy of nature, by a fear of interfering with processes no man could presumably understand, much less control. And to this serious handicap we must also add the Romantic liking for the formless, the incomplete, the unpredictable. You cannot very well demand form in the city when a generation of artists and art critics are in love with formlessness and expansiveness and go out of their way to denounce all restraints as academic.

It is not hard to point out the faults of the Romantic city landscape. The period is still too near us to have acquired the charm of antiquity or the atmosphere of another way of life. And because we are now in the midst of trying to find a new form for our cities, we are particularly aware of the obstacles that the Romantic heritage presents. Slums, decaying downtown areas, congested streets, the formlessness and immensity of every contemporary city are what we are constantly aware of. Nevertheless, we must try to do justice to the Romantic city landscape, and we can best do that by reminding ourselves what its innovations were.

The most conspicuous of these innovations was undoubtedly the introduction of nature into the city: not merely in the form of parks and gardens and landscaped areas in the immediate suburbs but also, and more fundamentally, in the increase of light and air and space. Whether the Romantic city succeeded in these efforts is beside the point. It is an endeavor we are still pursuing today. The second important innovation was the designing of what can be called intimate spaces — interior as well as exterior — for a culture that no longer relished so extensive a public life. A third feature of the nineteenth-century city landscape was the gradual elimination from the home of many traditional functions, so that it became a more intense, more private environment connected with our inner life and not with our life as members of society. And this, as I have suggested, led to the development of the last characteristic of the Romantic city landscape: its profusion of specialized functional areas — areas for amusement, for work, for study, for social intercourse, for sport, even areas for has never been practiced on so wide and imaginative a scale. It is a different kind of planning from that which prevailed in Europe in the sixteenth and seventeenth centuries, but some of the results are the same: a heightened awareness of aesthetic factors in the city landscape, a unification of architecture and urbanism, and a realization that planning is very much involved with how people work and live and enjoy themselves. In the Romantic city, planning all too often was a matter of real estate development or of administrative decisions. Our century is once again thinking of the social implications.

Another aspect of our Contemporary city landscape that resembles the Baroque is a fresh emphasis on the spectacular, the representational. The impact of advertising is by no means confined to the printed word; it not only lines our highways with billboards but also lines our streets and avenues with elaborate commercial or promotional architecture, and its techniques have invaded our recreation areas and even our dwellings. Our skyline, particularly after dark, is alive with impressive propaganda, and we do not have to be reminded that much large-scale architecture is an attempt to institutionalize commercial firms, or to humanize public institutions. If the Contemporary city is not a society of buildings, it is not, strictly speaking, a jungle any longer. It is a chorus of public relations experts, and it seems to me that representational architecture flourishes just as vigorously on one side of the Iron Curtain as on the other.

Finally, there is the growing revival of mass pageantry — world fairs, monster rallies and sporting events, the deliberate inflation of celebrations into what Professor Boorstin has called the pseudo event. We are increasingly besieged by the arts of illusion, of stagecraft, of interior decoration on a massive scale.

This rediscovered enthusiasm for public activity and pageantry is definitely Baroque. I find it interesting to observe how sociologists, urbanists, artists, and social commentators are increasingly delighted by the vivid street scene. Bleecker Street, the North End of Boston, Grant Avenue, the Mexican Quarter of Los Angeles or San Antonio, and of course the fiestas and market squares of all Mediterranean and Latin-American countries are held up to us for admiration. I undoubtedly show a reactionary point of view when I question the possibility of reviving the Baroque street scene in the United States. It is not that I object to it; it is that the public is no longer the same.

For better or for worse, the average European or American has become largely independent of the street. The notion that we can lead any significant part of our lives in public is an agreeable one, but I do not believe it is realistic. It is true that Baroque squares, the garden of the Palais Royal in Paris, and Vauxhall Gardens in London were in their time very efficient schools for manners and dress, and excellent places to acquire news and worldly wisdom. Indeed you do not have to have reached my years to remember the strict social discipline that certain fashionable streets in Europe imposed on everyone who walked down them. But those days are gone, and gone for good, and one of the reasons the street is no longer a place for acquiring a liberal education is that it no longer reveals the entire social order; it merely reveals the average unimportant citizen. I know of no European or American city where the street scene provides any such insight into the culture of the times as did the scene in any Roman piazza in the Baroque Age. It is not enough for the street scene to be entertaining. Albuquerque, near which I live, has a main street swarming with Indians, ranchers, Mexicans, farmhands, Mennonites, dry farmers, tourists, cowboys. But the street scene must be edifying (though I dislike the word) as well as entertaining, and that is precisely what our Neo-Baroque public pageantry is not and never will be. The explanation, as I see it, is simple. The population of our large cities is much too heterogeneous, and people are not there to loiter or show off, that is, if they are older than eighteen; they are going about their private business.

This is not to say that public gathering places are not needed. They most certainly are, and to a great extent the Neo-Baroque proponents are correct in demanding their creation. But they must be adapted to our less extroverted society. And this, it seems to me, is one of the important tasks facing the contemporary architect: the designing of suitable public gathering places. This is something that the Romantic city typically ignored, with the result that the average American city is a very lonely place for the stranger. Consider mid-town New York. Aside from Rockefeller Center and Bryant Park, both of them inhospitable in bad weather, there are no public gathering places appropriate to a large city. Except for the concourses of the two railroad stations, one of them doomed to destruction, the only indoor places where it is possible to foregather freely with other people are the lobbies of hotels, the waiting rooms of bus and airline terminals, and the public library. And the numerous public in search of quiet and repose is obliged to invade either the museums or libraries, or St. Patrick's Cathedral. Most Protestant churches are closed throughout the week. But the solution, as I see it, is not a series of pedestrian malls or more parks or sidewalk cafés or shopping centers or any Neo-Baroque revival but a totally new kind of public gathering place. I must repeat: it is quite unrealistic from the point of view of both climate and temperament to expect the Contemporary city dweller to find much satisfaction in open, free-for-all public places. We are not a homogeneous group; we do not derive pleasure from people as such, and unfortunately we no longer have much in common with every passer-by. That may still be the case in Naples, but in modern Europe and America we tend instinctively to form groups of compatible persons — stamp dealers, writers, tipsters, soldiers on leave, suburban wives in for a day of shopping. And speaking for myself, I see little point in trying to alter this state of affairs.

I strongly suspect that the new kind of public gathering place will be an enclosed, well-defined area, not only to exclude weather and noise, but to exclude by some kind of psychological barrier the enormous heterogeneous public, and at the same time to give these gathering places the character of a specialized precinct. I have in mind one such modern public area, the passage in Vienna under the Ring. It contains a number of stores and refreshment stands, and it has become the chosen gathering place for teen-agers. I see nothing wrong in this. On the contrary, I see it as an example to be studied for other groups in the city.

Thus the Neo-Baroque is definitely part of the Contemporary city; that we should have all gathered here to discuss urbanism and architecture is evidence of this. But the Neo-Baroque tendency is not the only one at work. We have another, more recent heritage, that of the Romantic city landscape with its feel for the sanctity of the individual and the individual environment. What is more, this Romantic heritage is now no longer confined to the upper and middle classes. It has become much more general throughout the whole industrialized world, and I can think of no better indication of its popularity than the fact that somewhere near half of the people in this country now own their own homes. Their title to that home may be precarious, and the home itself may be a tract house. Nevertheless, these domestic environments continue to multiply, and as long as they are a part of the American city landscape, we cannot expect to have a very animated or complete public life. So a second challenge to the architect who intends to help form the Contemporary city is to give serious thought to an up-to-date definition of the dwelling and its relationship to the larger community. The transformation of the American home as an institution is a very commonplace topic; we are always blaming something — communism, juvenile delinquency, corruption, materialism, poor church attendance — on the home as an institution. But how about the home as a kind of spatial design? Has it kept up with recent changes? Are we always aware of the role the home plays and does not play? Are we aware that the community necessarily changes when the home changes? The distance between dwelling and place of work is something we severely deplore, because we say that it destroys the community and that so much travel is an intolerable burden. Perhaps this is true; and yet it seems to me that it is precisely this remoteness from the workaday world — from the community as well as from the place of work — that the average American seems to value in his dwelling. The private environment becomes in a sense more and more private, further and further removed from all other aspects of life. It is my own belief that the automobile has, if anything, added a new dimension to our Romantic heritage of individual isolaton, for the car seems to be, much of the time, a microenvironment, a mobile version of the dwelling. When we are in it, even when we are on our way to work or in the crowded streets of the city, we are essentially detached from society, and what could be a better illustration of this than a large traffic jam? It gives the superficial illusion of a throng; in fact, however, it is a mass of individuals who are not communicating, who are not even touching, who have only one thing in common — an impatient desire to be moving. This is the lonely crowd that fills our highways and streets and gives to our cities the illusion of active social intercourse.

There is one final aspect of our Romantic tradition that shows few signs yet of disappearing; this is the area of specialized function. Just as every individual is fragmented into a variety of identities — wage earner, family man, citizen, and finally the solitary mobile individual, each with his own special environment — the modern city remains divided into many distinct quarters, each with its own type of activity, its own routine, its own organization. There are many critics of the urban landscape who deplore this compartmentalization, but it seems to be strongly entrenched in the modern city scheme. We have only to witness the resistance of a residential suburb to any kind of invasion — whether of an ethnic minority or a commercial enterprise — to be reminded that the Romantic tradition of the inviolate, one-purpose environment is still very strong.

It remains for the future to reconcile these two very different tendencies, the Neo-Baroque desire for public amenities and socially directed design, and the Romantic desire for the isolated experience in the isolated environment. This is not a field where I have any knowledge, but I have a strong suspicion that the solution will not be found by attempting to revive any urban form out of the past. I cannot see any value, for instance, in the more or less self-sufficient subcommunity, the neighborhood, the village within the city, which is at best a convenient arrangement of certain services. Whether we approve of it or not, we live in the midst of a collection of highly specialized urban landscapes; our lives and interests are scattered across a wide area, and the geographical bond has become an artificial one. I think that it is possible to foresee a city where there are centers of activity and leisure focused around those special functional areas rather than around the traditional facilities and institutions — church, school, shopping center. It is a matter of designing and planning these specialized areas so that they serve the wider public: communications centers, medical centers, amusement centers, educational centers. Jackson Square in San Francisco is a very modest example of what I mean. A section of town devoted primarily to one interest, one type of business, has here managed to dramatize itself so that it has become an attraction for many people. But it is not a neighborhood center.

Biologists sometimes make the distinction in the social forms of animals between those societies which occur through differentiation and those which occur through integration. Differentiated societies (like insect colonies) "all stem from one mother, and the distribution of work, the social interplay of the members of the colony is essentially the innate differentiation of blood relatives." (I am quoting here from Adolf Portmann's *Animals as Social Beings.*) In other words, they are organized according to predetermined castes into workers, soldiers, drones, etc., and it may be said that they all exist and act primarily to keep the society in existence. On the other hand, those societies which occur through integration are formed through integration of different ways of behavior. The individual members are drawn together for protection, for mating, or simply by some gregarious instinct. They do not surrender their individual freedom, however, and they establish their own territory and choose their own mate, both of which they will fiercely defend against the rest. To put it briefly, one form of society stays together; the other form comes together.

It is always dangerous, particularly for the layman, to draw comparisons between animal and human behavior, but the theory at least suggests two of the choices in urban philosophy

Technology and Urban Form

*The Influence of Changing Communications, Transportation, and Occupational Structures**

AARON FLEISHER

The idea that there exists in technology a potential capable of radically modifying the conditions of human existence has made prophecy a matter for common concern. In former times, when life and death were the only great changes noticeable or conceivable, the future was a drama to be played in the next world. Prediction, accordingly, was the proper function of priests. In this world, only the roles and the lines remained; the players were anonymous and the sets indifferent.

The sense of time quickened, however, when change became documented. A new mode of travel, a new means of communication or source of power made the shape of the immediate future a cause for debate equally in commerce and philosophy. But

*Dr. Fleisher's lecture was drawn largely from an article in *Daedalus*, Vol. 90, No. 1, published by the American Academy of Arts and Sciences, Brookline, Massachusetts. It was reprinted in *The Future Metropolis* (New York: George Braziller, 1961), and is reproduced here by permission.

these recent prophets were usually more concerned with the effects of technology on the particulars of their own interests. A synoptic view was rare, even until the immediate present. J. B. S. Haldane's *Daedalus, or the Science of the Future* and Bertrand Russell's *Icarus, or the Future of Science* were isolated examples.

To realize the larger view, however, is hardly a simple matter. One has to anticipate the potentialities of technology, as well as the course of all the other changes that flow independently from technology, then gauge the interaction of both kinds of change —which compounds the problem of prediction at least thrice. These compound predictions can be considered an example of what is called systems analysis. I suspect, however, that the kinship between such analysis and these compound predictions is too remote for much help. But it is a comfort to know that one is not alone.

The utopians should have contributed something to this problem, for, being concerned only with an ideal society and not with the historical process, they could bypass the more difficult part of the prediction and deal only with the interactions. But they ignored these, thinking it unnecessary to question the consistency of the society described and the technology prescribed. An organization tailored to a people which travels by dogcart and communicates by radio need not also fit one which travels by airplane and communicates by smoke signals. The omission is not a trivial one, even when the society is fully synthesized and then set in motion. Not every static society is a stable one. An important test of a utopian proposal, one that is rarely run, is its stability in the presence of perturbations.

To separate the influences technology will have on the city is an example of such a compounded problem in prediction. An estimate of the future of technology is a difficult but not an unreasonable question, certainly somewhat safer now than fifty years ago. We know more now; therefore the possibilities are easier to assess, and the present concern with limits (of devices, or principles, and even of knowledge) adumbrates an upper boundary to conjecture.

The city is a large, complex, loosely linked organization. Its equipment is bulky, immobile, costly, and obsolesces at a rate that is rarely measurable in smaller units than decades. Sometimes, the rate of obsolescence is even negative, since some equipment becomes more valuable with the passage of time. By contrast, research is no longer exotic, and its pace has become so quick that the distinction between science and engineering is difficult to maintain. The flows of urban and technological time, therefore, are not commensurate. In how many cities are the streets so arranged as to delight the motorist? And when they are modified, the expense is huge, the pain intense, and the conversion a compromise. Whatever the reason for the lag between these two kinds of time, it does exist, and therefore fifty years of urban history is equivalent to thirty years, at most, of technology.

This fact represents a dislocation in time. There is perhaps another dislocation in value. The gap between the capability and the usable product is an expensive one. Even if the economy were rich enough, the society might not choose to pay the cost of development. And when resources are finite, proper allocation requires some measure of desire and advantage. I prefer to avoid such market analyses, for they are enmeshed in matters of taste and policy.

By "urban form" I mean only the density of population as a function of locus in the city and the time of day. Such a definition ignores some kinds of experience entirely and treats many others lightly; but it does capture an important characteristic of the use of land, and it contains, at least by implication, some of the operational and structural constraints on the city. Moreover, to specify urban patterns in greater detail than future changes in technology can be anticipated would be a wasteful mismatch. Time is a dimension we have hardly mastered, and modesty, therefore, requires that all but the largest changes be temporarily set aside.

This definition of urban form provides a rationale for sorting technology by relevance. New foods and clothing, for example, are irrelevant. New products and materials, as a general category, are irrelevant. New industries, except in their locational eccentricities, are irrelevant. None of these is likely to modify the spacing of people.

At the other end of the scale of relevance are the possible devices that will replace or separate people, or move them and their products. These devices span distance and time, and therefore changes in transportation and communication are especially relevant. An inquiry into the manner in which technology affects urban forms might profitably be pursued by raising these specific questions: Are there any physical limits to growth? Will changes in communications and transportation favor any particular pattern of density? To what degree will the response depend on size and geography?

The Limit on Size

Some simple rules of thumb taken from demography suggest that toward the middle of the next fifty-year period a city of twenty-five million will be able to exist. Such a concentration would be unworkable if either external supply or internal distribution should prove too expensive. There is almost no possibility of an absolute failure. I assume that the entire population of the country will always be adequately supported. If there are no national shortages, then the external supply is a problem of import, and therefore of total channel capacities: port, rail, truck, and air. About five times New York's capacity is a reasonable estimate, and this looks easily attainable from the present capabilities of the large seaport cities, without any substantial increase in the unit cost. However, supply will not have to depend on present means. Capacity will increase as pipelines and airlines move more deeply into the freight business, and channels will be used more intensively as cargo juggling becomes easier.

As for supplying the city itself, there is enough food now to support the larger population, at least in this country. But the industrial and domestic uses of electricity per person have hardly reached the saturation point. The amount of power required, therefore, will not increase at the same rate as the number of people. Still, hydroelectric sources are not capable of indefinite extension. However large it may be, the amount of water in the atmosphere and on the earth's surface is finite. Whenever and wherever necessary, nuclear reactors can be used as supplementary sources, and these are likely to be used, as are conventional fuels, in thermal engines. Water, then, is a necessary component in the power-conversion cycle. Efficiency in its use is increasing, and the quality of the water need not be high. Location, therefore, will not be particularly critical, and where it is so, the capabilities for transmitting electricity will probably be equal to supplying urban centers from distant sources.

The amount of wastes that will accumulate will be monstrous, but by some chemical means they will be manageable. Radioactive waste, however, cannot be disposed of so easily, and while the problem will not become critical within the next fifty years, if and when it does, the issues will be much more involved than the continued growth of cities.

The atmosphere is also used as a sewer. To judge from the intensity of the present concern with this problem and from the current rate of clearing, I would think that the noxious output per person will be cut at least by the amount of the increase in the population. If these new people did not spread at all, then the urban atmosphere would be no more loaded than it is today. Any pattern of lower density would improve matters. However, no account has been taken of local geography and climatology. Los Angeles, for example, is unfortunate in both these respects. Some comfort can be gathered from the prospect that the meteorologist will in the future be able to prescribe the optimum distributions for fixed sources of pollution. The automobile will require a different tactic.

An adequate water supply will not be easily assured. It should be possible to collect more water from a wider area, store it with less loss in larger dams, and transport it more efficiently to greater distances. The need for water, however, will increase faster than the population will. In time, then, a time which may occur within the next fifty years, new sources will be required. The sea is one such possible source; the control of rainfall is not likely to add very much. The location of new sources will usually be critical, and therefore transportation costs will be important. There is not very much new that can be done with aqueducts, and it is difficult to concentrate water. It will be expensive, and in some areas its lack may deter growth.

By the end of the fifty-year period the city may number fifty million. (The linear extrapolation is far less in error than the initial value of twenty-five million.) A factor of two, in my opinion, will have no marked effect on the external supply. What of the internal distribution? The price of things includes the cost of distribution. When all other circumstances remain the same, a difference in price becomes a clue to difficulties in distribution. Within the metropolis prices are fairly uniform and independent of density, and between cities there are only small differences. One can guess, then, that the cost of internal distribution does not vary across a wide range of densities, and that density would have to be rather larger than the largest value now known before one need worry about distribution.

The Effects of Changes in Communications

Some description of the observed patterns of density is now in order. Most modern cities display a distribution of density of population that has a sharp maximum in one or several small central areas devoted largely to business, and a diffuse minimum, pock-marked with commerce, where people live. I take this to represent a real conviction, not a convenient compromise. In the main, people choose to conduct their business in an environment that offers the greatest possible number of personal encounters and to spread their family affairs over as much space as they can afford. We need not here account for this choice; it is certainly not the only possible pattern of living, perhaps not the best or even the most efficient. Given this fact, how will it be modified by changes in communication?

The larger purpose of present research in communications is to design systems capable of transmitting information with greater degrees of reliability, fidelity, capacity, economy, and distance. Wherever the density is high, which is to say where personal encounters are important, fidelity is particularly relevant. Short of transmitting the actual person, the next most faithful representation is his picture. Let us suppose this kind of transmission to be as common as the telephone is today and not much more expensive.

One could easily compute the many occasions when the television screen would be a satisfactory replacement for the person himself. If these were advantages, they would be relative. Where the replacement fails, however, the failure is absolute and therefore critical. What would be the legal status of a video presence? Would the courts recognize it? The salesman and the buyer might be unhappy with a picture, especially if their sources of information were also tactile or olfactory. Not that smell and feel are impossible to code and transmit; but the working solution will require time and money. Color transmission is easier, but it is still poor.

Are drawings to be examined? Can equipment be demonstrated by television? The surgeon cannot use it. Can the psychiatrist? How well can a multicornered conference be served? It may not be adequate for transactions that would terminate in a handshake — or a fist fight. Clearly, it would not suffice for encounters that culminate in an embrace. I do not know in how many contexts people and things are replaceable by pictures. Some are matters of taste and fashion, and perhaps the largest number of such substitutions will derive from this category. Yet even if these were many, the advantage to the entrepreneur might be ambiguous. He could argue that, having to meet with people at some time in his negotiations, he might well settle near them now and enjoy the advantages of both propinquity and television. The shift may be worth the cost of congestion.

The telephone was also a dramatic technological change and provides an enlightening parallel. It is a rather low-fidelity device, having only about one thousandth of television bandwidth. But there are still personal encounters it could replace. Instead, the net result seems to have been an occasion to increase density. Having acquired an efficient means for preliminary negotiations and routine instructions, many people, ordinarily on the move, remained fixed. Space was saved, and higher densities were made workable. Television may have the same effect. By itself, it is ambivalent with respect to density.

Pocket-sized portable transmitters and receivers are already available. These are low-fidelity, short-range devices — in effect, personal telephones — useful only where the density is high, which they would tend to increase. Communication devices do span distance, but that distance may be fairly small. They are not therefore technically trivial, nor are their services unimportant. A seat in the gallery plus a pair of opera glasses is not as good as a box, but it is tolerable; and the man who takes a portable radio to the bleachers is not silly. All these are also examples of congestion ameliorated without diluting density.

For the woman of the house, the television screen may replace several shopping trips — certainly for standard items — and thus become the new mail-order catalog. (But if the package is standard, I do not see why the telephone would not do as well.) The importance of the supermarket might then be reduced. Her children may be able to attend school by way of the television screen — but I doubt that she would consider it an advantage. The number of shopping trips to the central city is not likely to be affected. Neither Bonwit Teller nor Filene's basement can be surveyed by television.

The telephone has contributed to the exodus to the suburbs, but by itself it would have been powerless. A parallel means of transportation has to be available. With similar reservations, television might exert a similar influence. However, I doubt that it can be as effective. The difference the telephone created is very much larger than the added advantage of a television channel.

The Effects of Changes in Occupations

Twice a day on most days the city experiences a wave of density created by people traveling to and from work. Therefore, it is in order to inquire into what changes can occur in the distribution of occupations.

I think that we shall see automation increasing at almost all levels of activity. People have long since ceased being significant sources of physical power. They are now being displaced as sources of perception and judgment as well. We are acquainted with the automatic oil refinery. There may be very few processes of production that are exempt from an equivalent control. Nor do the possibilities stop with production. Machines now exist that are capable of assuming many clerical functions, admitting and filling orders, retrieving and filing information, keeping records and accounts. They are also capable of a large number of managerial functions, such as scheduling and controlling production, keeping and maintaining inventory, collecting and routing shipments. To some degree they are capable of replacing engineering and technical skills. How far into the realm of policy making these machines can penetrate is difficult to decide. For present purposes, however, the ultimate limit is not very important. The machine has demonstrated its ability to affect a substantial part of the working population.

Changes in the complexion of occupations will depend on the money available and the comparative advantages of the machines: neither pick nor shovel is entirely obsolete. By the end of the fifty-year period there may be a marked displacement of white-collar and blue-collar workers, certainly in the large firms and to a lesser extent in government. The machines will generate new occupations and increase the number of people in others; but they are also susceptible to automatic processes in their manufacture and, even more so, in their use and repair. In time, the balance may show a net loss in jobs, more probably in the central city; but the loss should not be very large. Many firms in the city will not be affected, because their operations, however varying, remain either too small or too specialized.

In another respect, the machines may provide occasions for an increase in density. Now that growth, accretion, and diversification have become almost necessary for existence, a good part of the business world has become a highly branched affair. Many decisions that are being made locally and individually will, because of the advantages conferred by machines, be made centrally and collectively. A convergence of the intermediate layers of administration and control within the city is therefore to be expected; but how this will modify the pattern of density is less clear. The decision to locate, which is now based on minimizing some combination of cost and inconvenience in travel and communications, will probably be sufficient only to distinguish one metropolitan region from another. With respect to these rationalizations, the metropolis is fairly undifferentiated, for it is not by its facilities for travel and communication that its parts are best distinguished. In the future these facilities may be manipulated to influence a particular pattern of change, but such manipulations will not be matters of technology.

The requirements of the machine itself contribute very little to the locational decision. The information on which it feeds can arrive almost as well by wire as by person. A communication node is thereby required, but it need not coincide with a maximum in density of population. When management does centralize, it will probably favor the core of a large city, but its reasons for doing so will be neither economically nor technologically compelling.

Computers will probably tend to displace people in the core of all cities. In large cities they will make for a concentration of business controls and, therefore, of people. In such cities, the net change may not be a substantial one. There are kinds of counterflows in which the smaller cities can also participate. Local production and management may be attracted by the probability of a decrease in the price of newly vacated space, together with the fewer people and less parking space required per plant. At first glance, automated industries, being less dependent on labor, would appear to be freer to locate at will, but by themselves their working force may be insufficient to form a community. The town that is dependent on one or two industries will probably be rare. I should guess that, parallel to the recent migration from farm to city, there will be a movement from small to large cities.

The greatest effect the machine may have on cities is an

indirect one. The human work load will be substantially decreased. To provide for the new leisure can become a proper part of public policy and therefore a substantial determinant of the form of the metropolis. The prospect is hardly novel. When Herbert Hoover spoke of a car in every garage, he was not thinking of the trip to work.

The Effect of Changes in Transportation

These will be sorted by scales of distance. Let us take in turn the central city, the metropolitan area, and a region of cities. The events in each scale are not independent and are therefore not cumulative; these scales are devices of convenience. Consider the last one first. The complex of American cities — their locations, their functions, and their sizes — was determined in part by the transportation facilities of the nineteenth century, the railroads and waterways. A new means of transport that is sufficiently good can modify this complex by altering function and influencing relative rates of growth. The airplane may be one such means. For this purpose trucks are not essentially different from railroads. Therefore, the future balance between air and ground transport is relevant.

I do not think that any aspect of surface transportation — speed, efficiency, cost, or convenience — can improve by more than a factor of two; the wheel was a wonderful invention that reached the height of its development around the first half of the twentieth century. There is now being developed a kind of vehicle (the British call it a hovercraft) that rides on a layer of compressed air a very short distance above a surface. The surface need not be particularly smooth, and water serves very well. This vehicle has the obvious advantages of requiring only a cheap roadway and, compared with other surface vehicles, of generating a smaller amount of friction.

Over a long haul, these conveyances look capable of the loads and efficiencies of large trucks, with somewhat greater speeds. At best, they appear to promise no advantage where the network of roads is dense and the traffic heavy. Within the metropolis, their principle may be applicable to mass transit, but the possibility is a rather faint one. I do not count these vehicles as effective influences on future patterns of density.

The capabilities of the airplane place it in another class. It has already cut out a large portion of passenger transport and is now moving into hauling heavy freight. An aircraft that can take off and land vertically and fly at nearly three times the speed of sound is not an unreasonable projection. The national economy may then come under the influence of a new scale of time and distance. The nearest big city, the nearest shipping node, the nearest supply center can be five times farther than it is now. A new allocation of purpose and place with respect to transportation may develop. The larger cities will profit more, but the effect of their location is more difficult to decide.

What will the metropolitan scale of travel be in time and distance? If a region is to be considered a metropolis, travel should be possible between any two points with some reasonable daily facility. I take "reasonable" as requiring standards of comfort, scheduling, and time en route at least as good as those now available. If fifty million people are distributed in a metropolis with the average density of population of New York City today, they will cover an area equivalent to a circle twenty-five miles in radius; the density of Los Angeles would give a radius of sixty miles. Since the outlines of the city are not circular, these distances are at least half as short as they might be. Surface transportation under the best of circumstances will require several hours to get some people to work. To keep travel time within two hours, the average speed would have to be at least doubled. This means that each vehicle, whether automobile, bus, or train, must have its own right of way as well as some form of automatic safety controls. These requisites are feasible but expensive. If commuting is to be restricted to surface vehicles, then, in the sense of an easy interchange of people, the metropolis will be limited in extent. I have mentioned only the journey to and from work; the time allowed for others may be longer.

Aircraft engineers believe that in time they can provide a

system of mass transit, with a cruising speed of two hundred miles an hour, at a cost near that of the present systems. As with other mass-transit systems, the critical parameter is the mass. If such a system works at all, we may again see cities growing radially.

An alternate possibility is the one-car, one-airplane family. Aside from the parking problem, this seems possible. Since the private airplane must grow up within the federal airway system, it will probably acquire a strong sense of discipline from the beginning. Planners will therefore have an advantage with the private airplane that they have not yet acquired with the automobile. Even if the numbers of such aircraft are modest, the traffic problem will be formidable, for it will require keeping tabs on the origin, location, and destination of all flights over the metropolitan area. Airway channels can be as expensive and offensive as the highways.

Patterns of density may be possible for an urban population of fifty million that are quite satisfactory and do not require the mobility that aircraft would add. In its most modest role, the airplane would supplement the surface system required by the enlarged city. That is how the automobile got started, but it was only because policy provided the roads that it could eventually determine the prevailing patterns of density. The airplane has somewhat the same potential, but the dangers are not quite similar. It is more expensive and more difficult to operate; it starts from a position of control; and we are no longer as innocent as we were when the automobile was young. This time we are likely to make different mistakes. That some form of aircraft may be a common vehicle neither commits nor limits patterns of density but rather increases the possible modes of changes and growth.

Technology is not likely to contribute very much to the solution of the problem caused by the crowding of people and vehicles in the city. Congestion does not behave like a simple symptom of malfunction; otherwise, its reduction would be largely a matter of adding capacity. A new road is the standard solution, but in fact it is often invalid because the subsequent traffic becomes even more intense. To blame the new imbalance on the growth of the city or on a redistribution of travel is a tacit admission that the channels are not passive participants in determining how the traffic will be shared. Therefore, congestion cannot be controlled by simple additions to the network of roads. In this respect, the network of highways resembles a system with destabilizing feedbacks.

Suppose nothing is done about congestion. I do not think people will fall into a state of shock or fly at one another's throats. They will jockey for position, try different devices, make many experiments. Some will find equivalent solutions. Some will give it up and busy themselves in other profitable ways. Some will persist and get through. Some will lose everything. I do not know the proportion that will collect in any of these categories. If the last one comprises many, then we shall be sad, for we shall have been wrong. We should have done something. If the first category comprises many, then one or more transportation systems will have been devised, and we ought not to have said that people have become umbilically attached to their cars. If the second comprises many, then we shall have discovered new urban forms. If the third comprises many, then life will hardly have changed, and we shall have found that not all aspects of congestion are pathological — indeed, some may prove capable of existing in an agreeable homeostasis. But that state of grace cannot be attained by the application of technology alone.

Aside from the complexities of the problem if we consider only the mass of people and vehicles that must be moved, the maximum channels available, and the speed and amenities required, it becomes apparent that any uncompromising solution would violate the principle of the conservation of matter and the incompressibility of people and things. Technology has been variously invoked — wistfully, petulantly, or indignantly — to do something, as if it were possible to arrange five people and their impedimenta in the space occupied by one person. Proposals that turn in some manner on the size, organization, and ownership of vehicles and on the limitations and exclusions of travel do not pose difficult technological problems. All of them are soluble now. The debate that congestion has generated really hinges on questions of policy. I doubt whether there is any solution that will not in some sense proscribe someone's freedom to travel or that will not essentially modify the city.

Patterns of urban density and congestion are related: given the state of technology, we cannot specify either one independently of the other. Chronic congestion is a characteristic of cities, and I suspect that technology has been used to realize patterns of growth at maximum density, which is to say at maximum congestion. This policy was not a necessity but rather a choice from among other alternatives, however unconsciously made.

When technology was primitive, hardly any other alternative was possible. An automobile does not fit this choice easily because at one end of its trip it becomes almost immobile, and at the other, too mobile. It shares the former disability with other vehicles during other times. The streets of ancient Rome were also too narrow to bear the traffic. But the latter disability is a new event. The city at present may exhibit the first occasion in history of a society suffering from an excess of local mobility.

The determination of modes of travel is a matter of policy, but technology can contribute much to making them easier. Nothing radical can be expected by way of new vehicles. In heavy traffic, within a distance of ten miles, only a form of surface travel seems feasible. The largest advantages in this scale will probably derive from the elaboration of controls. These are the devices that will permit the most efficient use of the facilities. To design these controls would require a knowledge of traffic ranging from the micromechanics of congestion to the optimal properties of transportation networks in the large. The degree of control, however, would be a matter of policy. It can be as tight as the controls imposed on aircraft or as lenient as a set of street signals responding to local traffic. By themselves, controls are ambivalent with respect to patterns of density.

Summary

An inadequate supply of water seems to be the only condition that may stunt the growth of cities. In all other respects, a city of fifty million is a reasonable extrapolation. The future capabilities of communication are not likely to favor any particular form of the city. Automation in production and administration will change the profile of jobs and the length of the workday. The effects may be greater on the smaller than on the larger cities. All cities will be faced with the problem of providing for the increase in leisure.

Aircraft may become the dominant mode of transportation over long distances, in which case the relative growth of cities will depend in some measure on their position in the transportation network. If the amount of time devoted to local travel at present is to be maintained, then the span of large cities in the future makes it likely that aircraft will become a necessary component of metropolitan travel. If uncontrolled, this use of aircraft will encourage diffuse and formless growth. Local congestion, however, is not a technological problem.

The patterns of density within a city appear to be largely independent of technological developments. I think we should be unhappy if it were otherwise, for the fight for control is difficult enough as it is. Technology is now sufficiently versatile to meet most reasonable specifications. We need no longer wait and wonder.

The Ecology of the City

A Plea for Environmental Consciousness of the City's Physiological and Psychological Impacts

IAN McHARG

The modern Western industrial city is probably the most inhumane physical environment made by man for man. I think it will take the best efforts of modern medicine and social legislation to alleviate the abuses that the physical environment imposes upon us. Although less brutal than its nineteenth-century precursor, the city of today is more extensive and more toxic. I suggest that, with all the improvements that have occurred during the last century in the social environment, that is, in the aggrandizement and distribution of wealth, the physical environment has not proportionally improved but has retrogressed. The strenuous efforts of urban renewal, public and private alike, laudable though they may be, have contributed only islands of new construction, and the city remains anarchic, squalid, and dysgenic.

In this situation, I am searching for form. I want to envisage the modern city as a noble and ennobling place, but I do not see it emerging as a result of the criteria by which the planning process operates. Are these criteria adequate to the task of describing or prescribing? The summary answer is "No." Planning has become dominated by economic determinism in which basic human objectives — health, beauty, community — have been assumed to be unmeasurable and are therefore discounted. Convenience and growth are the goals; efficiency and money are the criteria of excellence. I have been seeking alternative determinants of urban form, and have found the views of the natural scientist, particularly the ecologist, more illuminating than any others. It is my primary purpose here to advance ecology as a science whose perceptions are of profound importance in solving the problems of the city. A distinguished economist, Kenneth Boulding, has proposed that economics be subsumed under ecology. This may be a future prospect, but it is not a present reality. For the moment, it is necessary to advocate the ecological view as an independent and complementary discipline.

Some of the ecologist's principles may, on first examination, appear rather simple, but I believe they have some relevance to our discussion. I should like to offer a comparison, which is not to farfetched, between the earth and the human body. The adult human body is composed of some thirty-seven billion billion cells (at a very rough estimate). Every one of these cells has a capacity to grow, to specialize, and to multiply; it has its own metabolism, its own life, and its own death. Similarly, one can think of the earth as a world life, the biosphere, in which all organisms and all communities have roles comparable to cells, organs, and tissues in the human body. When one takes a view of this sort, destruction is at once proscribed, because the idea of a world life as an entity in which all parts interact induces restraint in the act of self-mutilation. This is one of the first conceptions of the ecologist.

The ecologist is concerned with organic systems and their relation to the environment. A functioning, interacting system composed or organisms and their environment is called an ecosystem. Ecosystems are energy systems, depending on energy from galactic and solar sources. The energy is transmuted through photosynthesis and finally lost through entropy. Nutrients are cycled and recycled through organic systems. Organic systems are themselves depletive, and in order for them to function, there has to be reciprocity; for example, the waste of one organism is consumed by another, and, in turn, the waste disposed of by the latter is consumed by yet another organism. This process of reciprocity is called symbiosis.

The ecologist is concerned also with the economy of nature, and this he measures in terms of the amount of energy used in a system, and lost through entropy — the work performed by the organisms, and the load-sharing of the organisms.

Another object of the ecologist's study is succession, that is, development and adaptation in time. The word "niche" describes an association of microorganisms and organisms, which share loads and have reciprocal relationships, in a certain environment. The process of succession, the degree to which plants and animals are succeeded by other plants and animals, in association, in the same environment, leads finally to a conception of climax. This is the framework in which the ecologist examines organic systems.

I have to confess that these theories are incompletely and imperfectly described, and I am uncertain to what extent they can be applied to our area of concern. But I shall make an attempt.

Imagine, for a moment, the earth as seen by a man in space. He sees the earth as green with the verdure of land, and green with the maritime algae in the oceans. He perceives it as a green celestial fruit. As he looks more closely at this celestial fruit, he sees it has blemishes that are brown and black and gray, and from which spread dynamic tentacles. The observer, of course, concludes that the blemishes are, in fact, the cities of man.

Let us begin by thinking of a major city, about thirty miles in diameter, such as New York, and another area, of the same diameter, that includes hamlets, trees, plants, and meadows. If we could cover this area with a bell jar, or a giant Fuller's geodesic dome, we could allow light to pass through it unchanged, while preventing the passage of air. If we applied the dome over the city of New York, the inhabitants would die of asphyxiation within about twenty-four hours. If we put the dome over the countryside, composed of hamlets and fields, the people in this area would be unaffected. The reason for this is fairly simple. Given an appropriate density of animals and plants, there will be a reciprocity between oxygen and carbon dioxide. Animals—including human beings—breathe in oxygen, breathe out carbon dioxide; plants consume carbon dioxide, breathe out oxygen. A balance of animals and plants would ensure a closed cycle of oxygen and carbon dioxide. There would also be a water cycle, a carbon cycle, a nutrient cycle, and so on. In the case of the city of New York, the oxygen would be exhausted in a very short period of time. I do not wish to carry this idea too far, but I think it is salutary to believe that a city may be a concentrated toxicity, and that there is something productive in the notion that one can isolate the physical processes in a city and determine the degree to which they either enhance or inhibit life.

Another ability of the ecologist, as inheritor of the Darwinian-Wallace tradition of evolutionary biology, is to see the relationship between process and form in a clearer way than almost anyone else. Once upon a time, architects used to say "Form follows function." This was a kind of manifesto, illustrated by inorganic systems such as utensils, planes, and rockets. But if one notes that this was being proclaimed at a time when Darwinism had existed for almost a century, and sciences such a morphology were well advanced, it seems, in retrospect, almost an infantilism. If one examined organic systems, I think that one would be persuaded to adapt the statement and say "Form expresses process," or better still, "Process is expressive."

Biologists can determine a great deal about the role of the species, its location, and its adaptation to environment from the aspect of the species. Looking at the chambered nautilus, one can tell a great deal about the organism simply by observing its form. One looks at coral and sees this organism as a society and a community. The beehive is equally expressive as an organism in terms of a society.

These analogies are perhaps oversimplified, and as such are

barely acceptable, but I should like to offer one or two other examples of form expressing process that might provide insight in our search for form in the city. One of the most beautiful examples to my mind is a deciduous forest. Most people look at a forest and see it as a sort of randomness of green, but the ecologist knows that the distribution of the plants, their shape and relative size, and the period at which they flower and fruit are enormously expressive. Indeed, one could determine almost all the important things about the distribution and flowering periods of the plants from their form. The ecologist can draw arcs that indicate the time at which different plants come into bloom. Flowering and seeding are periods of maximum chemical activity and require a maximum amount of sunlight, which is the source of energy.

Recall that hepaticas and snowdrops and all the smallest plants tend to flower earliest in the spring. The reason for this is that they can have at that time all the sunlight they need, because the herbaceous plants, shrubs, and trees are not yet in leaf. The next group of plants to flower and seed are either the herbaceous plants or the shrubs. They, in turn, while casting their shade upon the smallest plants, do not yet receive any shade from the taller trees. They are then followed by dogwoods and redbuds, which are still unshaded by the larger trees, and can absorb the necessary amount of sunshine. Finally, the tallest trees of the forest spread their canopy and cast their shade on the plants and trees beneath them, while having access to the sunshine they themselves need. The morphology of the forest can thus be understood in terms of cycles of plants related to periods of sunlight. If one examined the root systems and nutrients, one would see evidence of the same process. The forest, which is at first seen as a mass of undifferentiated green, in fact, has specificity and is an extraordinarily expressive statement of an ordered system.

It is difficult to find examples of form expressing process in physical systems because either they are too complex, or they are part of geological systems that have matured over a very long period of time. It is hard to find a process in nature that is compressed in time. However, there is one example that I came upon very recently, and I am still delighted with it. It is the forming of the sand dune near the ocean.

This is a process that can be understood very well, and I cannot think of another example in which process is more clearly expressed by form. If a beach has an inclination of more than 5 per cent and less than 10 per cent, the action of the waves will pick up particles of sand and deposit them. In a very short period of years, the sand will be deposited to a point at which it remains above high water most of the time. This deposit of sand will, of course, offer an obstruction, and still more sand will be added to it, until it takes on the aspect of a dune. Portsmouth Island, south of Cape Hatteras, is such an example of a dune in evolution. A single dune has been formed, as yet without vegetation. If the dune reaches the height of nine or ten feet, marram grass will appear on the lee side. The marram grass, carried by tides, will immediately start to stabilize the dune. This particular grass thrives on being submerged by sand, and its root systems may grow to lengths of six feet or more, stabilizing the back of the dune. Raised above water, some of the sand dries out and is blown by the wind to the far side of the dune, and a second dune is begun. The first dune is called the barrier dune or the primary dune. In the trough behind it, marram grass appears on both sides and may reach the crown of the dune and even climb down its seaward side. This process continues until there is a plain or trough after the second dune, which may vary in width from twenty feet to several hundred feet. Another dune is then formed on the bay shore. We now have a cross section of a beach: a barrier dune, a trough, a secondary dune, a flat trough, then another dune, and then the bay.

Of course, plants volunteer. First of all comes the marram grass, then other herbaceous material, some woody material, and finally, in some instances (as at Buxton, Cape Hatteras), there may be oaks and pines. This form will sustain itself over long periods of time. It takes about twenty-five years to accomplish, which is a very short time in terms of geology. The sand bank, or island, is formed and is stabilized by a succession of plants.

All the elements of vegetation could be identified by some limiting factor: salinity, brackish water, exposure. The ecologist can identify the plants in terms of limitations within which they can exist, the environments to which they have adapted, their association and succession. One can see, in the function of all these variables, a form that is expressive. Through the eye of the ecologist, one can perceive this process very clearly. Perhaps this is still too simple a process to be analogous to the city, but I think it hints at a type of examination that may be relevant to the study of the city.

There is another process, on a larger scale and less complete than that of the sand dune, that I should like to discuss. I shall describe a river basin that I have had the opportunity to study closely: the Delaware River Basin, which encompasses the Catskills in New York State, a large section of Pennsylvania, a small section of Delaware, and some of New Jersey. Confronted with the necessity of coming to terms with land-use planning for this area, landscape architects selected the cycle of water as a means for examination. This again may be too exclusive; nonetheless, it is a valid device by which one can study process and see expressive form in this process.

If one thought of a river basin in terms of water only, one would start with the water cycle of evaporation and precipitation. But one can specify places where movement of the water occurs. One can identify the upland sponge, the Catskills and the Poconos, as the areas in which the highest precipitation occurs, the point from which most of the water in the basin originates. One can also identify the separate roles of the agricultural piedmont, the flat land and the valleys, the estuary marsh or sponge, and the aquifer. No surface water exists without ground water. We know that the aquifer, the underground water in New Jersey, is the single largest source of pure water on the eastern seaboard, but it does not exist unto itself. The aquifer exists only insofar as it is recharged from rivers and in turn recharges them.

The upland sponge is an area in which snow falls. It is a great reservoir of snow and, therefore, a great reservoir of water. The forests in this area have something of an ameliorative role. They act as a battery containing water and as a mechanically restrictive device to slow the movement of water to the lowlands. The agricultural piedmont is a great water consumer, but it is also a great water battery. The amount of water that is contained in all the living plants during the height of the growing season is prodigious. The degree to which the estuary acts as a sponge during tidal flood is measured by the amount of sphagnum moss present. This moss can absorb about 300 per cent of its own weight in water before it is saturated.

If one looks at the rivers and streams themselves, one finds some differentiation. The water has a particular role. Riparian land, that is, the land bordering a river or stream, has the function of preserving water purity. Flood plain zones are those areas which are frequently inundated, which people persistently occupy, and from which they are repeatedly extricated, wet, muddy, but heroic.

The upland sponge, the agricultural piedmont, the estuarine marsh, the aquifer, the rivers, and riparian lands all have intrinsic functions. If you examine a region such as the Delaware River Basin and locate these areas, you find that you have covered a rather substantial part of the whole region, somewhere between 50 and 60 per cent. You also find that you have produced something like a negative development map. Add that to your socioeconomic determinants! Before you locate new towns and developments wherever you please on the basis of economic determinism, add this parameter to your planning. See what intrinsic functions occur in this apparently undifferentiated green space, and observe the degree to which these intrinsic functions can coexist with the proposed new developments.

There is another principle that I should advocate here: that of the coefficient of runoff as a planning determinant. The Delaware region has a commission, formed by federal-state contract, that has been given a mandate to plan for water within the whole region. The army engineers have produced a flood-control plan for them, which is based upon a volume of water at maximum flood. As a result of the plan, there will be a number of main stem dams along the Delaware, the Schuylkill, and the

Lehigh rivers. The plan will not succeed unless the coefficient of runoff (the amount of water that runs off and the rate at which it runs off) remains constant in relation to the maximum flood. The army engineers are in the dam-making business, and I doubt whether they are overly concerned if New York adds another fifteen hundred miles to its perimeter at an average coefficient of runoff of 80 per cent, which may well spoil the entire plan. They are probably prepared to build dams from now until doomsday. Some responsible citizens, however, might wish for the plan's success. This again is a matter of reciprocity. In any constituent watershed, there should be a coefficient of runoff that, at maximum flood, would produce just so much water flowing into a major tributary or into the Delaware itself.

Let us suppose that a town is to be built in this watershed for between fifty and eighty thousand inhabitants. In this case, the coefficient of runoff would be transformed from about 5 per cent of the maximum flood, if the land were in forest, to between 50 and 80 per cent, and a great deal more water would be precipitated out of the watershed at the critical period. Two courses of action would be possible. The city planners could say, "Let it happen. If there is a flood, the engineers can go and build another dam," or they could say "No." The reasonable view would be this: if we are going to add many square miles of urbanized land and increase the coefficient of runoff, either we must take a certain amount of land out of agriculture and put it into forest, or we must make some compensating arrangement in another watershed. Accepting the fact that urbanization increases the coefficient of runoff and increases the incidence and intensity of future floods, we can compensate for this by practicing land use that entails a low coefficient of runoff. I believe that the scientific theories in existence today enable me to show you how to design the Jersey shore in such a way that you need never fear another flood. If the soundest principles of biology, ecology, and oceanography had been applied to the treatment of the Jersey shore, there would not have been a catastrophe in March 1962. It was as a result of the gross stupidity of breaching the dunes, destroying the vegetation, and poverty is the range of physical and social diseases. The East River section has fifteen times as many juvenile delinquents as the Park Avenue section, ten times as much alcoholism, three times as much active tuberculosis and infant mortality. These figures undoubtedly have parallels in Chicago, Boston, Philadelphia, San Francisco, and other large cities.

The Midtown Manhattan Study did not include a survey of the physical environment, but it is clear that environmental conditions correspond to conditions of wealth and poverty. The amount of space per individual; the opportunity for privacy, safety, relaxation and rest; quiet, cleanliness, and fresh air: all these are important factors affecting physical and mental health.

An Experiment in "Pathological Togetherness"

In this experiment, a pathological state was induced in rats by conditions of density and pressure in their environment. Doctors John Calhoun and John B. Christian made independent studies of animals in the wild and in the laboratory to discover endocrinal responses to environmental conditions. In particular, they identified density and consequent social pressure as an important factor in pathology.

In the experiments conducted by Dr. Christian, breeding couples of rats are placed in an "extensive" environment, that is, a large cage, with ample food and water, and material for making litters. The rats breed, and the population rises. As it begins to reach half its maximum, the rate of natural increase declines. (Dr. Christian realized that there is a "maximum," determined, not by available food and water, but by density and social pressure.) This is first observed in intra-uterine resorption, smaller litters, deformity, failure of lactation, and cannibalism. Next, disease is observed in the adults: heart disease, arteriosclerosis, kidney disease, and cancer. The population then declines almost to the level of extinction. Examination of the appropriate organs revealed stress as the major cause of these diseases, and, in turn, stress appeared to be the result of increased density.

Dr. Calhoun has been preoccupied with the incidence of mental disease resulting from increasing density, and has found that disease and "antisocial" behavior affect a larger and larger proportion of the population. It gives one pause for reflection that the diseases studied in these experiments with rats are similar in nature and in circumstance to those suffered by twentieth-century urban man.

Pathology is not considered, from the orthodox viewpoint, a necessary concern of members of the planning professions. Yet an optimum division of responsibility would accord to architects, city planners, and landscape architects, at least in part, the creation of an environment of health.

There are several other important environmental considerations I should like to mention. Pollution of the atmosphere and hydrosphere has stimulated a superabundance of scientific literature and a paucity of action. It is seldom a planning consideration. Atmospheric ionization has a much smaller literature and has generated no action. Yet, it has been found that atmospheric pollution, toxic materials, and carcinogens, together with positive ionization produced by combustion, not only cause disease but diminish the capacity of the organism to react.

There is a story of how Lewis Mumford found a policeman in New York who had been standing at the same corner, directing traffic for years and years. He suddenly fainted one day and was taken to a hospital. It was found that his tolerance of carbon monoxide had been greater than anyone could believe possible. Perhaps we are all increasing our tolerance of carbon monoxide, but I do not know that this situation has any compensating advantages. The simple idea of the South Sea Islanders of planting ten trees when a child is born is a sensible one for people who depend upon oxygen. The knowledge that a fountain produces negative ionization is useful to people who tend to suffer from an excess of trotting (*not* running!) and who probably need more negative ions.

Studies of sensory overload reveal that there are limits to the amount of information that can be accepted by an organism. Beyond this limit, stress is caused, which may take many forms. Studies carried out at the Eastern Psychiatric Hospital in Philadelphia show that many people confronted with sensory overload respond by "filtering out" the overload to such a degree that they suffer hallucinations as a result of sensory *underload*. The physical environment of the city is generally so chaotic that people have to "filter out" in order to survive, but if there is too little for them to grasp, they finally filter too much and become understimulated.

If stress is, indeed, a cause of susceptibility to disease, then we must seek the form of city that will reduce stress. Rather than producing some sort of median of not much stress, not much stimulus, and not much tranquillity, we must strive for maximum intensity of stimulus and maximum tranquillity and repose. We must be certain that architects, city planners, and landscape architects do not subscribe to the perpetuation and increase of that which is life-inhibiting. We are not fulfilling our role if the city can exist thanks only to advances in medicine and social legislation. It is necessary for us to find a modern city, not an eighteenth-century city with unsatisfactory additions and alterations, but in every sense a modern city. I suggest that there may be a possibility of finding a form for this city through the perceptions of the ecologist.

Environmental Architecture

A Team Approach to Design on a City Scale

VICTOR GRUEN

In coining the phrase "environmental architecture," we are attempting to describe a new professional approach by architects — an approach that expands their activity, their experience, their knowledge, and their working methods, with the aim of shaping the entire man-made and man-influenced human environment.

Wherever architects or architectural critics or historians meet, we hear a lot of moaning about the present sad and confused state of architecture. The profession of architecture is said to be in a state of chaos, confusion, and aimlessness. Some architects are engaged in a feverish search for a new style of twentieth-century architecture, and we hear about "brutalism," "functionalism," a new "romanticism," "purism," and so on. Some architects work in one specific so-called style, while others manage to change their stylistic approach from project to project and sometimes have on their drawing boards, simultaneously, projects following the principles of opposite stylistic expressions. The result of this hectic search for a new style is what is described aptly in architectural magazines as "chaos."

To try to create a new style deliberately is about as hopeless a task as trying to catch a rainbow. A style is an elusive thing, never achieved when it is consciously sought. What are really being created today are not styles but fashions and fads as they prevail in the millinery and ladies' apparel business.

Real styles are not consciously created. They are discernible only when the eyes of the viewer are directed backward at least fifty to one hundred years.

It might very well be that a new style in architecture, in the sense that Gothic or Baroque was a new style in its day, cannot be created any longer. My reason for this pessimistic statement is that one of the most important factors for the growth of a style is *restriction*. In the past there were the restrictions imposed by the availability of materials and construction methods within the specific region and period in which a style flowered, by the specific tasks architecture was asked to fulfill (which were in the past limited to public structures and those commissioned by the ruling classes and the church), and by many other considerations that existed at the time and place of the formation of the style.

Twentieth-century science and technology have robbed us of these restrictions. We can overcome extremes in climate by insulation, heating, and air conditioning. When we design a building, we have a multitude of building materials and construction methods to choose from, and technology has advanced to such a degree that practically every shape and form can be created at any place in the world and under any climatic conditions. Distances between all parts of the globe have shortened dramatically, and the web of communications is so tightly knit that what is built in Chicago today can be discussed in an architectural magazine in Tokyo next month. The range of the activities for which an architect can design has been significantly widened.

The staple food of the architect is no longer the church, the palace, the mansion for the rich, or the public building; his diet is now an extremely varied one where building types and the economic status of the users of his buildings are concerned. Thus it would appear that the search for style may be a wild-goose chase, leading to frustration and waste of creative strength and intellectual power.

Should one thus conclude that architecture has no exciting and exhilarating mission in our times? Nothing, in my opinion, could be further from the truth. The mission of architecture in these times of mass production, mass consumption, population explosion, and urban growth lies in a completely different area than it did in times of a relatively static social structure.

In order to attack the new problems that are awaiting the architect's attention, we have to realize clearly what they are. We must recognize that in a society in which wealth is no longer held by only a few hundred or a few thousand but is shared by a growing majority of the population, in an era in which, in developed countries, the overwhelming majority of the populace has become urban, architecture has to widen its horizons; it has to switch its attention from the individual structure to the total environment.

While maintaining his earlier role of *architekton*, master builder, and directing spirit of all those who participated in the shaping of an individual structure, today's architect must fulfill the functions of a creator, guide, and co-ordinator for the vastly larger number who are participants in shaping the man-made and man-influenced environment. His new working team, therefore, consists not just of designers, engineers, and contractors but also of economists, sociologists, administrators, lawyers, political leaders, transportation engineers, and so on. The question may arise, of course, whether the architect, through his training and education, is prepared for this tremendous and complex task. The honest answer is that he is inadequately prepared, and I know that other speakers at this seminar will deal with the problems of training the architect in order to prepare him better for his new role. Yet in spite of this inadequacy, architecture is the only profession that can, and therefore must, shoulder the greatly enlarged responsibility. It is the only profession that has historically, in creating structures for human use, always assumed the leadership position in a team. Why, then, from the architect's own point of view, is it necessary to switch his attention from the individual structure to the over-all environment? The reason is simply that within our complex society the most brilliantly designed individual structure, because it is so totally dependent on the environmental conditions surrounding it, can become, and indeed often does become, ineffective. If the architecture of the individual structure as a personal expression is ever to become meaningful again, the task of reshaping the existing human environment must first be tackled.

What are the outward expressions of our chaotic human environment? Though our cities are growing dynamically, their growth is an unhealthy, cancerous one. Instead of mature growth within, it is an uncontrolled, sprawling, and scattering growth along the periphery of urban organisms, a growth that destroys agricultural land and the beauty of landscape and nature, a growth so unplanned and rapid that public services remain far behind in furnishing water and sewers, roads and schools. While the countryside is being covered with this "urban fallout," the most important seats of urban culture and civilization, the historic city cores, are rapidly deteriorating. Beset by the dangers, noises, and fumes of mechanized surface traffic, they are being deserted by their inhabitants and denuded of daily visitors. Thus our metropolitan areas are reminiscent of doughnuts, with all the dough on the outside and a hole in the middle. This centrifugal movement results in a cultural, civic, and political impoverishment through destruction of the centrally located places that were, in the past, the main generators of cultural, social, civic, and political fervor with only widely scattered, inadequate facilities within the widely spread suburban cultural desert to take their place. Other devastating results are the waste of millions of man-hours necessarily spent in nerve-shattering transportation from home to work and back, and the ultimate bankrupting of municipalities. From an aesthetic point of view, the effect of this centrifugal movement is to create, on the one hand, undistinguished, deteriorating, and neglected urban cores and, on the other, vast, boring, characterless, and commercialized regional suburban zones. Suburban highways, with their array of gas stations, hot dog stands, billboards, and cut-rate stores, are identical from Maine to Mississippi and from Boston to Los Angeles.

Already there are in formation continuous areas of that suburban scatter aptly called "megalopolis," one reaching from Boston, Massachusetts, to Washington, D.C., one located in the Chicago and Milwaukee area, and one reaching from Santa Barbara, California, to San Diego, California. These are areas that, if a halt is not called soon, will be of everlasting sameness, void of any interruption by landscape, and plagued by a steady deterioration of their original existing historic and dynamic urban centers.

In the last ten years the chaotic growth and development of our urban areas have awakened the public to an alarmed awareness of its dangers. There is willingness, indeed an eagerness, now to call a halt to the continuous waste of one of our natural resources, namely, land. There is a deep undercurrent of resentment against the ugliness and inefficiency of our public environment, against the waste of time in traffic on congested highways, and against the lack of values in urban life. The climate is right for a decisive attack leading toward the improvement of man-made environment.

We in Victor Gruen Associates believe strongly in the new field of environmental architecture, and we are, to the extent of our ability, trying to practice what we preach. Though I am aware that, measured by the size of the total task, our contribution is an extremely modest one, I believe it would be worthwhile to describe how we approach the new problems of architecture through our organizational setup, and through teamwork with others, and to try to illustrate the effects of our effort by discussing a number of specific projects in the field of environmental architecture.

Fig. 1. FORT WORTH, TEXAS (1–5)
Fort Worth before rehabilitation.

Fig. 2.
Forth Worth tomorrow, after completion of Victor Gruen Associates' plan. A loop or belt road, accessible from the freeway, encircles the new city core. From the belt road, turnoffs penetrate to car-storage structures and bus terminals close to the heart of the city's central section. Comparison with Fig. 1 *shows that existing major physical assets remain intact.*

Fig. 3.
Downtown Fort Worth today.

Fig. 4. (See top, facing page.)
Study by Victor Gruen Associates for the nine-block downtown area seen in Fig. 3. *All surface traffic has been removed and the pedestrian is king, although the essential physical characteristics of the area are unchanged. By elimination of cars and trucks from the central business district over 5,000,000 square feet have been gained — 3,500,000 for malls, walks, and parks; 2,000,000 for new productive purposes. (Gordon Sommers photo)*

Fig. 5. (See bottom, facing page.)
Seventh Street, Fort Worth, transformed into a pedestrian mall. (Gordon Sommers photo)

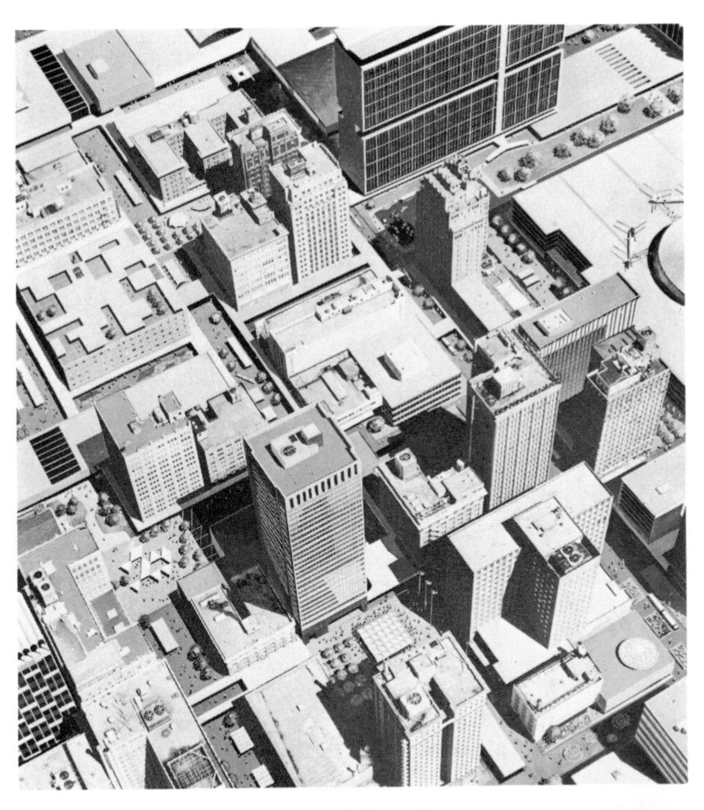

COMMERCE
GARAGE
COMPLETED

Fig. 6. RANDHURST, CHICAGO, ILLINOIS (6–7)
Three levels in Randhurst, Chicago, a shopping center by Victor Gruen Associates. (Gordon Sommers photo)

In order to be armed for the task that we must fulfill in the widened field of "environmental architecture" as we understand it, we have built up a broad organizational base. Within a tightly knit organization we have an architectural department, a planning department, a structural, civil, mechanical, and electrical engineering department, a transportation engineering department, an economics department, an interior design department, and a graphics department. The activities of the organization are guided and directed by seven partners, each of whom performs a double function: he heads one or more departments and is also in direct charge of a number of projects. Thus, each partner is responsible for all phases and types of work within the particular project he heads as partner-in-charge, but his particular training and experience are also available to all other projects. In this manner, each project benefits from the totality of the experience and talent available in the

Fig. 7.
The open entrance to the Fair in Randhurst, with children's play sculpture in use in the foreground. (Gordon Sommers photo)

organization, while the client is assured of the continuous attention of one of the partners.

About forty associates work closely with the partners as co-ordinators and in other leading capacities. They are also responsible for co-ordinating work with our staff of about two hundred, and with outside consultants. The existence of the various engineering departments, an economics department, a transportation department, etc., does not preclude, on larger projects, working with outside consultants in these fields. We feel, however, that the existence of these departments within our own organization enables us to co-operate with outside consultants in a more intelligent and effective manner.

Where the scope and character of our projects are concerned, our only specialty is that we oppose specialization. Thus our projects range over every building type from small shops to regional shopping centers, from residential projects and civic

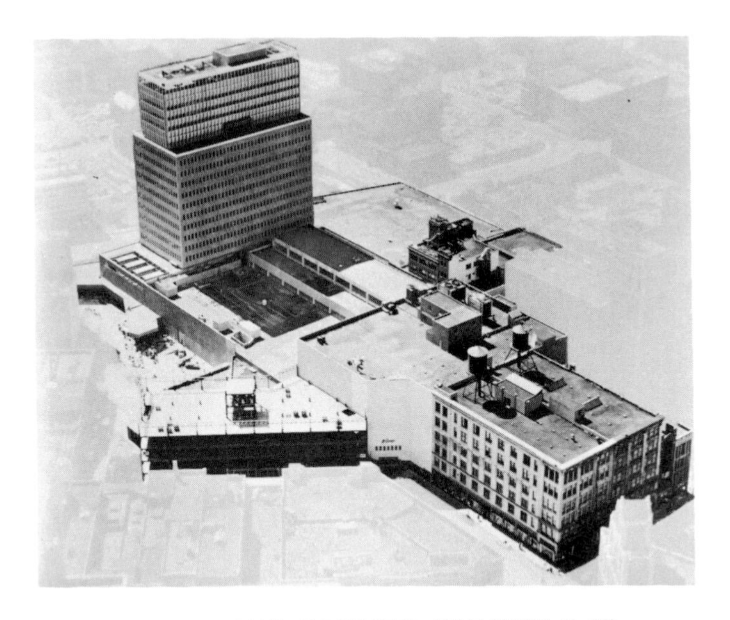

Fig. 8. MIDTOWN PLAZA, ROCHESTER, NEW YORK (8–12)
Midtown Plaza, Rochester, New York, showing the complex of structures in relation to the surrounding downtown area. The large new building in the background combines offices and a hotel, with a terrace restaurant on the fourteenth floor. The buildings in the foreground, two department stores, have been enlarged and modernized.

structures to new communities, downtown revitalization, city planning, regional planning, etc. As far as their size is concerned, they range from projects costing $50,000 to those costing $200,000,000.

Historically speaking, of course, we did not start with the overall task of environmental architecture but worked toward this aim from small beginnings, starting with private houses, interiors, shops, and stores, steadily widening our range over the last fifteen years. The first projects that permitted us to express our ideas about environmental architecure were regional shop-

Fig. 9.
Diagrammatic section of the new building in Midtown Plaza, Rochester, showing all levels; Victor Gruen Associates, architects.

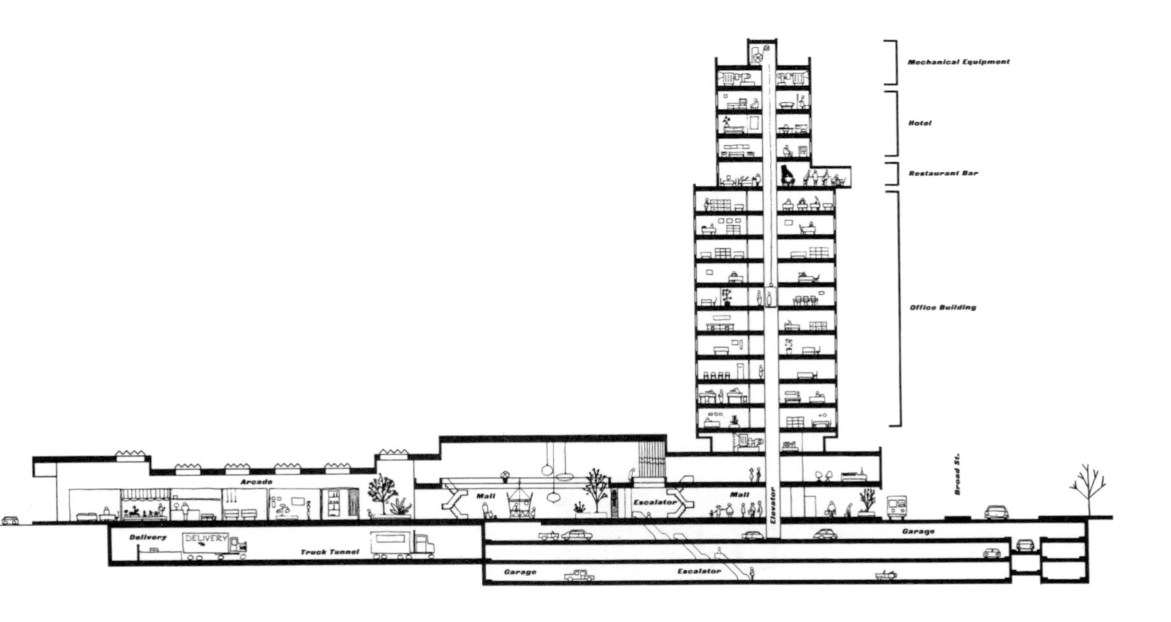

Fig. 10.
The mall in Midtown Plaza, Rochester, with crowds gathering to watch and listen to the Clock of Nations in action. (Gordon Sommers photo)

ping centers in which we attempted to create more than a grouping of stores. We strove to create a type of urban cluster within sprawling suburbia that could act as a crystallization point for social, cultural, and civic activities. The work on these regional shopping centers gave us an opportunity to test on large virgin pieces of land the planning concepts that we felt approached effectively the problems and potentials created by twentieth-century technology and sociology. In a sense, they were the workshops in which we forged certain planning principles that we later applied to existing urban complexes or newly planned communities.

Projects concerned with environmental architecture demand an unusual amount of dedication, perseverance, and patience.

Fig. 11.
A corner of the mall in Midtown Plaza, with escalators (which connect all levels) in the background and an advertising kiosk and other furniture in the foreground. (Gordon Sommers photo)

Fig. 12.
A sidewalk café just off the main mall in Midtown Plaza, Rochester, New York. (Gordon Sommers photo)

Fig. 13. FRESNO MALL, FRESNO, CALIFORNIA (13–15)
Street scene in Fresno, California, before revitalization. (Tidyman Studios photo)

Fig. 14.
View from the same spot as Fig. 13, *today. (Tidyman Studios photo)*

Fig. 15.
The new mall at Fresno with benches, fountain, minibus, and, in the distance, the clock tower.

Fig. 16. EAST ISLAND, NEW YORK (16–17)
The projected development of East Island, or Welfare Island, New York, by Victor Gruen Associates. Photograph of model superimposed on air view of East River.

Yet we feel optimistic about the outlook for the effective role of environmental architecture. When we started, our plans moved in a vacuum because of the lack of public understanding and public interest and, most of all, a lack of tools and instruments for their implementation. Since then — and we feel we have made our modest contribution to this achievement — tools like urban redevelopment legislation have been created and refined. Many improvements are still needed before these tools will fit the task. But there is at least talk now about urban transportation legislation, federal funds for the improvement of rapid transit, legislation to protect landscape, agricultural land, and nature, and so on. We have just started to work on a project

Fig. 17.
Diagrammatic section of East Island development.

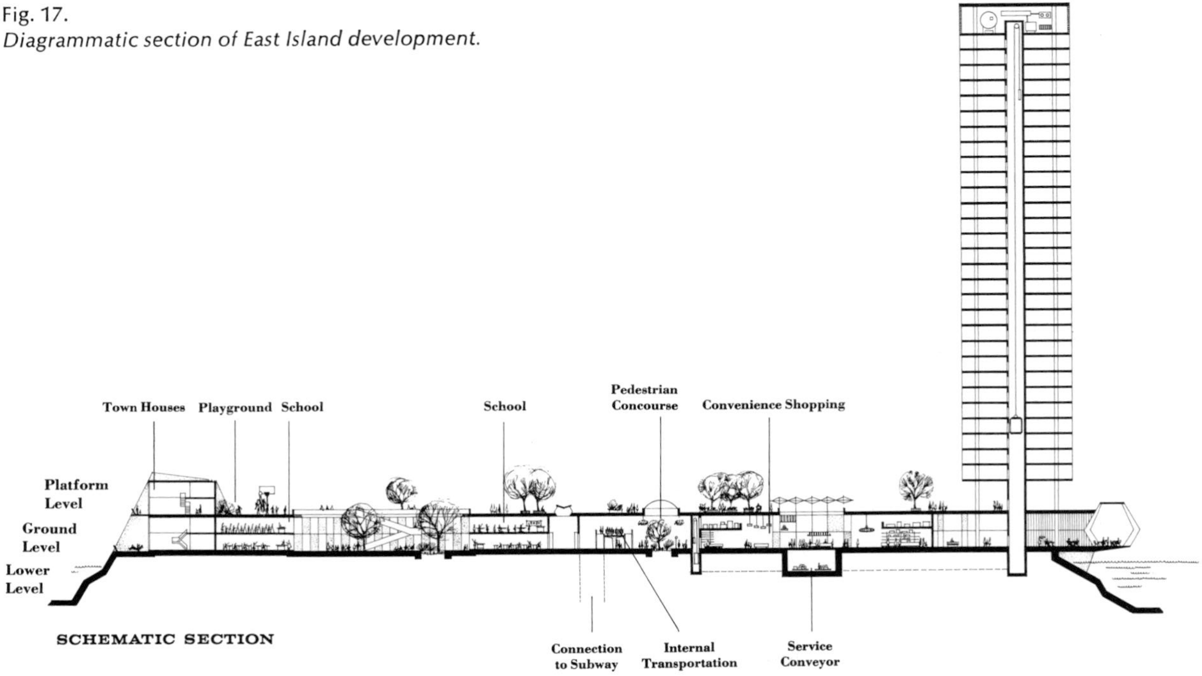

Fig. 18. BOSTON, MASSACHUSETTS
The downtown area of Boston, Massachusetts (surrounded by white line), whose revitalization is one of Victor Gruen Associates' more recent projects.

that concerns the comprehensive reshaping of the core area of one of our larger and older cities, Boston, and here we are encouraged by the fact that ways have been found to bring about a close co-operation between the government and private enterprise.

We are, of course, deeply aware of the fact that scientific and technological development have put into the hands of mankind not only the means for improvement of the man-made environment but also those for its total destruction. Believing in life and believing in people, we must hope that reason will prevail and that mankind will not destroy itself. If reason prevails, then the madness of armament competition will have to subside; and when that happens, vast energies will be released for an all-out battle for the improvement of the places in which man lives. This, in our opinion, is the task and responsibility of architecture in the second half of the twentieth century.

The Urban Renewal Architect—Dr. Purist and Mr. Compromise

Parables from the World of Urban Renewal

JAMES J. HURLEY

The fact that most of the speakers here are distinguished architects and planners makes me wonder if David Crane has not cast me in the role of the Devil's Advocate, an emissary from the Powers of Darkness who rule so dominantly outside the groves of Academe, especially in the cities. In any case, I should like to hold the metaphor and speak about the good and evil spirits of the city that haunt the hell of urban renewal.

I think it highly appropriate to speak about the "Powers of Darkness" because, in my view, as in that of Lewis Mumford, the purpose of the city is not a human one but rather a divine or demoniacal one. According to Mumford and others, the historical origins of the city were to serve the purposes of the gods. I quite believe this. If we examine the contemporary city, or any city of the past, with any degree of critical objectivity, we must conclude that the city was not created to serve man's purposes.

Fig. 1. SPLENDOR OF THE GODS (1–2)
The god of Power has few splendors to equal that of the boulevards of Paris. His cavalry sweeps insurrection from the streets; his archway proclaims his glory for all to see. (French Government Office photo)

As Lewis Mumford pointed out in his recent book about the city, the village came into existence during the paleolithic or neolithic age, when man's primitive mate desired more security for herself and her offspring than the nomadic huntsman's life afforded. The village was therefore the first expression of man's communal instinct and woman's desire for collective security. Each family unit had its own independent economy based on crude harvesting, and all villages were alike. The city, which made its appearance several thousand years later in the valleys of the Nile and Euphrates, was also a human community, an expression of man's communal instincts, but it had a different purpose. It functioned in a totally different manner.

Fig. 2.
The god of Greed has few splendors to equal that of Manhattan. Great are his temples there, and great the human sacrifice therein. (New York Convention Visitors' Bureau photo)

Fig. 3. SPIRITS OF THE CITY (3–5)
The goddess of Apathy allows the god of Greed to pollute the air of the industrial city . . . and great are the benefits therefrom.
(The Times *photo)*

Fig. 4. (See top, facing page.)
The wheel, intended for man's benefit, is put to the service of the goddess of Sloth, and the human shank shrinks because there is no need to walk in the modern city. From Victor Gruen and Larry Smith, Shopping Towns USA *(New York: Reinhold, 1960), p. 20.*

Fig. 5. (See bottom, facing page.)
The glories of modern civilization proclaimed at every turn give birth to the goddess of Boredom, who will reign forever and ever.
(Rondal Partridge photo)

CLUB
Health & Bea
Save 25-4
VITAM
IN
RUBBE
STAM
Give Kentucky's
Full fifth decanter
...no extra cost
West
QUORS
VAN
formerly
WINE CELLAR
Fred's
PLACE
Warren's
Ladies
Children
DUCTS
PIZ
El Real
WIN. W.
TOMPKINS
&
Company
3944
DRAUGHT
V ODKA
GIN 2.79

According to Mumford, the huntsman, technologically unemployed by the somnolent village economy of planting and harvesting, grew weary of the dull domestic routine and discovered a new purpose — the creation of the city, which was to be the dwelling place of a god or gods and the hunter-predator turned king or priest to serve the god. According to this thesis, the city had its foundations in heaven so that the gods might dwell on earth. The historical purpose of the city has never been, and is not now, to serve man but rather to serve some god, or thing outside man, some inhuman purpose. It is very important, therefore, that you and I, who are concerned with any aspect or function of the contemporary city, should recognize the theological origins of the city, and its inhuman purposes.

You may be unwilling to admit the existence of gods or demons in this enlightened age. You may say that, of course, in the days of Memphis, Nineveh, Babylon, Ur, and Carchemish, the citizens of those places believed in the actual presence of gods dwelling in the citadel. You may be unwilling to admit that the later cities of Athens, Rome, and Syracuse held dieties within their walls. But was not Jerusalem sacred to Jehovah? And did He not promise His people to dwell forever therein? How often in the Old Testament are we told how the ancient Hebrews built their city at the command of Jehovah so that He might dwell among them? And did the Egyptians not carry this to its ultimate? Each Pharaoh god dwelt in the flesh on the banks of the Nile near the site of his pyramid tomb, and thousands upon thousands of slaves dwelled about him and spent their brief lifetime building his tomb. And with his interment his city disappeared, leaving behind a necropolis barren of life or activity, while a new city grew up around a new Pharaoh god. The ancient Egyptian city is perhaps the most striking example of the thesis that the city is not conceived to serve the purposes of man.

You may say that it was ages ago when men lived in fear, ignorance, and superstition. Let me say that spiritually men live today no less in fear, ignorance, and superstition than did their ancestors. The modern commercial city is no less a dwelling place for gods than was ancient Carchemish.

Who are the gods? The familiar deities of the modern city are Greed and Power. They are wicked gods, or demons or spirits, that compel urban man's mind and heart and too often motivate his actions. Of course, these spirits always existed. They were manifest in motivating the Pharaohs of Egypt as well as the financial operators of modern Texas. The reason is simple: there is a little of the gods, good or evil, in every man, and therefore it is not surprising to find homage paid to the wicked gods in our contemporary cities. So, for the purpose of my thesis, let me call these gods Greed and Power, the motivating spirits of Mr. Compromise.

What about the motivating spirits of Dr. Purist? They are the gentler and nobler spirits of Beauty, Art, Harmony, Reason, Balance, etc. They are just as real as the wicked spirits, and personally I find them more attractive and agreeable. But somehow their gentle natures are hardly a match for Greed and Power. You are less likely to find them in the great cities; they tend to seek refuge in more pastoral surroundings, in the ivory towers, and in the groves of Academe. Nevertheless, they do appear from time to time in the city, almost always in the company of an architect.

The city does not pay much homage to the ideals of Dr. Purist — lip service perhaps, but not homage. I do not scoff at Dr. Purist or at his ideals. I laugh at his naïveté when he suggests that the wicked gods of Greed and Power abdicate in favor of his gentle spirits. No city, to my knowledge, exists today where only the good spirits of Dr. Purist reign supreme. There have been communities, especially in America, established in the name of Brotherhood and Beauty, but sooner or later the gods of Greed and Power hold the mortgage. That is no reason to abandon faith in the good spirits of Dr. Purist; it is merely a reason to reckon with the dark powers of Mr. Compromise.

Therefore, if you or your students wish to make a mark in city planning, you must approach it rather schizophrenically, recog-

Fig. 6. THE ANTIGODS (6–7)
The servants of the gods dwell in cosy togetherness, hating the cities of the gods. (Peter Blake photo)

Fig. 7.
The sinister spirit of the Expressway threatens the city of the gods, and the servants of the gods shall destroy the temples of the gods. (Peter Blake photo)

nizing both the good and evil motivation behind the building and running of the contemporary city. By no means abandon your visions, but do not expect to find them fully realized in the city as we know it. Unless you see the theological side of urban renewal and city planning in these terms, you are doomed to a state of incomprehension and frustration.

Do not despair, you followers of Dr. Purist, even though there is no victory in sight, even though everywhere you look the city gods of Greed and Power are triumphant. You can live — a little — and occasionally score a point or two for the good spirits of Reason, Harmony, and all the other deities of Dr. Purist. Be content to live with the bad spirits as well. They have been around a long time and will be around for a little while longer. Only they have the power to destroy themselves — and their cities — which I think they may do very soon.

The god of Greed in that imperial city of New York is rivaled by the god of Power in Moscow and by the gods of Greed in Peking and London and Tokyo. And when these gods have a falling out, you will have one of the greatest opportunities for urban renewal that you can imagine.

How, then, is this theology, or demonology if you wish, to be applied in your life as a city architect? You cannot be an urban renewal architect without encountering these spirits and their high priests, their worshipers and devotees. To the god of Greed belong the market place, the bankers, the mortgage lenders, the landlords, the developers with all their talk about economic feasibility, return on investment, and rights of ownership. To the god of Power belongs all the apparatus of government with its myriad agencies, the FHA, the URA, the HHFA, the building code, the master plan, etc. And one of your saddest frustrations will come from the servants of Power or Greed who will invoke the names of the good spirits of Dr. Purist, such as Economy, Public Welfare, Safety, etc., only to support some inhuman demand by the god of Power.

Do not despair. Has man not outwitted the gods since the time of Homer? He can still do so even in the field of urban renewal. Let me cite some examples.

The Gods Receive Sacrifice

A certain city eradicated a sixty-acre slum area under Title I and offered it to redevelopers. There were four contenders; three local groups each having a builder and real estate operator were the prime movers, and the fourth contender was a well-known developer from out of town. The local groups employed local architects; the professional developer employed an architect with a national reputation in association with a local architect. In time all submissions were submitted to the redevelopment agency. The award was to be made on the basis of architectural merit and price. The three local products were dull and ugly, with a large portion of the land devoted to commercial use. The out-of-town developer's submission, following the desire of the redevelopment director, was clearly outstanding, with its mixture of high-rise buildings and row houses, and with only a small fraction of the land used as commercial space. The director of urban renewal, who is a Dr. Purist, wanted very much to award the project on the basis of architectural merit because it met all the objectives of his plan. But the best design carried the next-to-lowest price tag for the land.

After several months of hesitation, the director made a courageous decision and awarded the project on the architectural merits because it was in his power to negotiate the contract. Then all hell broke loose. The contending local real estate operators banded together to rid themselves of the outsider. They cried for the director's scalp and brought such pressure to bear that the god of Power stirred. The local director called in the successful developer and told him the only way he could put the deal through was to match the high bidder's price and sacrifice some of the quality of the plan. The developer reluctantly agreed. At this point his architect became nearly hysterical because his plan was sacred and could not be changed.

The problem was simple. How could all the gods be satisfied a little? To the god of Greed an additional $150,000 was sacrificed; the god of Power was mollified because the local operators could not cry thief! However, it took a little time to satisfy the gods of Dr. Purist. The sacred cows of proportion, scale, etc., were going to be violated because in order to absorb the added land cost the architect had to increase the number of housing units by a hundred, and this meant going from nine to fourteen stories in each of two buildings. The architect threatened many times to resign before he would yield; I was the consultant to the developer on that job, and I told him that if he did not add fifty units to each of his buildings, the project would never be built.

He yielded, and I am happy to say that the story has a happy ending. The buildings are built, and the architect met me not so long ago and admitted he had been wrong about the optimum height limitation for aesthetic reasons. One of the disappointed local real estate contenders has built new commercial space across from the development and is reaping a harvest he tried very hard to destroy. The director has a completed project better than he had ever dreamed of. The only sad note is that none of the local construction men got the job of building it.

In this case all the gods, both good and wicked, received some sacrifice from the urban renewal team, and the project was built, perhaps not absolutely according to the ideals of Dr. Purist, but not according to the demands of Mr. Compromise either.

The Rivalry of the Gods

A portion of a renewal project was designated for low-rise town-house development of five hundred dwelling units of two- and three-bedroom size. This was called for by the master plan even though for this specific project it was just barely feasible. The developer, when he realized what this meant in terms of investment, recoiled and sought to have his redevelopment contract altered. But the renewal director had committed himself to one of the good spirits, and his ideal was to bring the "solid middle-class" family back to the city, but solid middle-class families with children do not live in high-rise apartment buildings. Therefore, the town house was decreed.

The master plan, a sacred cow in this case, was very much cherished by the god of Power — as much as the developer's profit is cherished by the god of Greed. Clearly, some accommodation had to be found. The master plan had one basic flaw in it, which was the assumption that family units in low-rise developments need not be detached or semidetached houses. I quickly pointed this out to the developer and his very ingenious architect, who came up with a row-house design that accommodated the five hundred family units on considerably less land than was originally contemplated in the master plan. With the land area thus saved, we proposed to build an additional three hundred units of high-rise apartments, thus meeting the requirements of Economy and incidentally satisfying the god of Greed. The director, as a representative of the god of Power, was satisfied because it met his objective, which we all agreed was a good objective. It seemed that we had satisfied all the gods. But — the god of Power has many minions, and one of them was the Evil Building Code, which called for certain minimum lot areas for family homes, whether row houses or not. We outfoxed the Evil Building Code by classifying the row houses as a multifamily apartment building; but then we ran into the wicked regulations of the fire department, which called for a four-foot continuous fire-resistant overhang connecting all apartment entrances that had an exterior entrance. By this time we had learned to trick the gods. We outfoxed the fire department by getting our buildings classified as individual row houses for fire purposes only. And so we presented different faces to different minions of the god of Power, and in the end man triumphed over the wicked gods of Greed and Power.

How the God of Greed Hurt Himself

A certain developer to whom I acted as consultant was awarded a project of twelve hundred housing units in one of the Eastern cities. Against my advice, he proposed to build the entire project at once. The $400,000 that he estimated he could save on the construction would sustain the large number of vacancies that I predicted in case my idea of the market absorption was correct. I estimated that the market would sustain a net gain of ten to twelve tenants every week, meaning at least a two-year rent-up period. There were two pressures on him. One was the potential saving of $400,000, a pure dollar gain, and the other was the pressure of the city's renewal director to complete the project as soon as possible. Here was a case where the gods of both Power and Greed were in accord, on the surface only. My prediction proved surprisingly accurate, and the project sustained a loss in excess of $700,000 in the thirty-month period it required to rent. You see, the gods are not omnipotent. The god of Greed, with a little help from the god of Power, defeated himself.

The God of Greed Is Shortsighted

Not far from here, in the city of Detroit, there is an urban renewal project called Gratiot-LaFayette. Its sponsor, the late Herbert S. Greenwald, consulted me several times about it. My only contribution to it was a suggestion to do a rather extensive and consequently costly landscaping job around the low-rise "town houses" to give privacy to the tenants. Even though "Economy" was invoked, I suspect it was homage to the god of Greed that caused my suggestion to be rejected; and, irony of ironies, Greed was not served, because lack of privacy was one of the chief reasons why these buildings were never fully rented. I have not seen this project in two years, but unless the developer spends some money on landscaping, this beautiful urban renewal plan by Mies van der Rohe will never be utilized. Here, then, is one instance where the power of the god should have been opposed, in order to serve his true purpose; sometimes, ironically, the god's purpose is coincidentally the same as man's. I must add, though, that Herbert Greenwald more often listened to the good spirits of Dr. Purist than to the bad spirits of Mr. Compromise; in his tragic passing, urban renewal has lost a valiant spirit.

What morals can we draw from these modern parables of the city gods? The important conclusion that I have drawn from my experience in the field is that the wicked gods of Mr. Compromise are not so terrible or omnipotent that they cannot be outwitted at times, with a point or two scored for the good spirits of Dr. Purist. In your conduct as urban renewal architects, therefore, you must recognize the presence of the wicked spirits, learn their whims and their weaknesses, and while giving due recognition to them, continue to serve the noble spirits of Dr. Purist, within the context of the real city, the city of actual conditions. Continue to "make no little plans," in the words of Daniel Burnham; you may even "stir men's blood," but you must do it within the context of real conditions, which are frequently not conducive to good planning and good architecture. Remember the real hazards of being too much either Mr. Compromise or Dr. Purist. And, best of all, be yourself.

If your client is either Power (government) or Greed (the developer) and you serve him slavishly with no regard for the gentle spirits of Dr. Purist, then you will end up as a hack, unworthy to be called an architect. Though your plans may be built, they will hardly renew the city.

If your client is really your own ego, you will probably end up an architect of literature, the quintessence of Dr. Purist, with your files of unbuilt dreams. Certainly no cities will be renewed through your cerebrations, and you will not dare to call yourself an urban renewal architect.

You will therefore need character and temperament as well as your art; and it is not the character of Hector or Ajax but rather the character of Ulysses that will make you a hero in urban renewal.

Architecture in Change

European Experiments Pointing a New Direction for City Design

ROMALDO GIURGOLA

To regard as retrogressive the changes in the structure of human settlement that have occurred in the course of time has become commonplace — even more commonplace when the causes are urban density. For the origin of such a negative attitude, we must look back more than half a century, to when the attack upon the slums in the ever-expanding cities was opened by the new forces of sociology.

At that time the urban phenomenon began to be the subject of investigation at different levels, revealing the city from within for the first time in history. Planning at the theoretical and practical levels was realized, and a quantity of observation helped to orient planning to the functional organizations of urban activities, as an operational discipline indispensable to the new configuration of the city. In fact, the city as an organism, which already existed in the intuitive state for the architects of the ideal city, began to receive a more conscious and precise form that is fundamentally a derivation from the Spencerian notion of society. The methods of the natural sciences were applied and the old systematic theories abandoned.

This is the fertile ground in which the ideas of Patrick Geddes and in our time the high historical sense of Lewis Mumford grew and flourished. We should never forget that these ideas have been for years the inspiration of architects and planners in every part of the globe — definite proof of their universality in spite of their Anglo-Saxon origin. More recently, we have been treated to a variety of urbanistic philosophies — some of deterministic, economic character, others more specialized in the sociologic-geographic technique.

Let me explain at this point that different words denote "the art of building cities"; and because they are not synonyms, confusion often arises. Their differences reflect different attitudes toward the art. German *Stadtbau* and the English *town planning* seem to emphasize the material aspect of the urban construction. The French have *l'art de bâtir les villes*.

The French word *urbanisme*, in its English form, *urbanism*, is the one that I shall use, and I urge that it be adopted since it has a more comprehensive meaning. Besides denoting the material act of planning, it includes the entire complex of disciplines whose objective is the life of urban aggregates. It is a case similar to the distinction between environment and milieu. *Urbanism* means "the general study of the conditions, motivations, life needs, and development of the city." Thus urbanism, although not an exact science, is still a discipline whose aim is an architectural synthesis of all those values which represent the urban aggregate in the broadest sense of the word. That is, urbanism is an art.

Urbanism is not a modern art; on the contrary, it has guided the formation of civic life for centuries. The industrial revolution presented new technical problems and created new needs; in the attempt to offer particular answers to them, the unified vision of the city life was lost. Then recently, a more vital interaction between technical culture and politics has developed, and in the specific case of planning there has been the growth and deepening of historical observation. By "historical observation" I mean an experience related and dimensioned to the facts in their continuity and complexities caused by their ever-changing development. This is not to be confused with the search for historical parallels, which are only of relative and more often than not academic interest. I should like to remind you that the technical consideration of new facts, such as the statistical appreciation, while necessary for the approach to the problems from outside, often has been incapable of demonstrating the value of the dynamics of facts and events that characterize the situation of civic life.

With these premises in mind, I shall try to detect some basic changes in cities and the apparent directions and tendencies of the formal expression of them. It will be necessary, however, to take a quick glance at the origin of modern urbanism and some of the transformations that the human aggregate has gone through.

The early denunciations of material misery caused by the cancerous growth of slums started back in the second half of the eighteenth century; indeed, the English state of affairs was only one aspect of a new situation that became general in Europe and America, with visible consequences in the structure of the cities and the new political and economic aspects of the modern state. When we look back on the words and deeds of the early reformers, we feel that they were incapable of co-ordinating and resolving, on a common ground of action, the moral problems, and the corresponding material ones, of Victorian society.

In fact, the split was assured from the start. On one side, there was architecture with its paraphernalia of aesthetic ideas and ideals; on the other, there was the strictly operative problem, characterized by technical dryness. The prevalent plan was the gridiron — the mercantile town.

The very refusal by Owen and Fourier and other theoreticians to consider a co-ordination of the human rapport within the existing city and their hopes for a solution free of limitations and compromises in an ideal society outside the city are indications of the unwillingness to reach for the proper means of natural continuity. Since their ideas represented a ready opportunity for speculators, the internal problem remained unchanged; Welwyn Garden City and Letchworth were indeed cultural and literary expressions. So, with their failure to approach the problems from within, were the other garden cities.

I do not intend to elaborate on these aspects of urbanism and what seems after all a failure of historical penetration. I should like rather to focus attention on the fact that with the deep alteration of social structure, economic life, and cultural patterns a physical change took place in the symbolic areas of the city. Such areas, especially in Europe, generally coincided with the old political and mercantile center in which the new was added to the old according to a process of integration and absorption that almost never led to the total destruction of what existed. This happened for different reasons and to a lesser degree in America, where the cities (at that time Boston) had just started their intense life. Of the many integrations of the old center and the new, the most notable is certainly the great axis in Paris: the Louvre–Tuileries–Place de la Concorde–Champs Elysées–Place de l'Etoile axis. So it happened in Berlin though in a less agile and elegant manner, while in London these integrations appear in a very particular way, independently of any preorganized geometry, in that peculiar dense urban form that is the zone of the City, comprised in the sweep of the Thames between Lambeth and Blackfriars Bridge.

It is true that evolution of this sort, pivoting around the older monumental works, had been realized in earlier times — it is enough to remember the Rome of Sixtus V — but by the end of the nineteenth century these monuments really constitute the foundation on which the center of the city became transformed, with a character often totally different from its previous one. However, in the cities of the nineteenth century there is little of that sensitivity toward controlled spatial relationship which seemed an almost instinctive characteristic of the fifteenth and sixteenth centuries. In its place a geometric schematism by large parameters is substituted; a scheme that is obedient to a generalizing and positivistic philosophy, which had a predilection for an open urban form, with no limits, where often the merely large takes the place of the great, and ornamentation the place of deeper celebrative architectural expressions.

In spite of the aspiration to the monumental, a real detachment of the general public from an authentic creative intent was revealed in this trend. The center of cities was formed to express a new civic order in a hierarchic scale of attributions sustained by a dominant will that by now was completely impersonal. It is interesting to notice how, in direct contrast to the principle of *laissez faire*, the urban center of the nineteenth century was influenced in an even deeper way by the uniform sentiment of an anonymous crowd, with no ecologic differentiation, incapable of recognizing a vital limit in the urban space; the nineteenth century was ready to impose, as a uniform symmetrical scheme, façades repeated with monumental monotony, and streets running on without end.

The Baroque city was a city of cluster satellites saturated with energy released from the core of a major building. The civic architecture of Rome and Paris of the nineteenth century, by eliminating the architecturally modest linking sections between monumental structures familiar to the Baroque Age, prepared for that progressive dissolution of provincial values in the community life that would slowly lead to the decisive crisis of our century.

We are able today to recognize the sufficiency of those realizations, their dignity and monumentality. No real substitute has been found for that rich density of nineteenth-century architecture in the civic centers. When theoretically all the residue of provincialism has been eliminated, a so-called "pure architecture" will still be incapable of expressing the power, vigor, and stability embodied in the nineteenth-century civic center. Therefore, in our city core the nineteenth-century structures emerge from the deep transformations that occurred in the last fifty years and impose themselves as an indispensable

Fig. 1

Fig. 2. MONUMENTAL AND ANTIMONUMENTAL (1–2)
The polarities of large-scale planning are represented by the Square de la Tour Saint-Jacques (Fig. 1), *created as one of the focal points of Second Empire Paris, and the new Freie Universität Berlin, designed by Candilis, Josic and Woods* (Fig. 2). *Napoleon III's "square," isolated by the broad streets that were to help provide "simplified defense on days of riot," belies its English name in that it is less a space for pedestrian enjoyment than a setting for a monumental vertical feature in the cityscape. Berlin University has no dominant vertical features at all and provides free circulation at two levels between largely standardized units of teaching accommodation, thus expressing an open and democratic society as surely as Second Empire Paris expresses a dictatorship. (Square de la Tour Saint-Jacques from J. Alphand,* Promenades de Paris; *Berlin University model, photograph by courtesy of the architects)*

past in our civic life. The success of Penn Center hangs upon the existence of City Hall, the loss of which would have been irreparable.

In the lapse of time between the two wars a huge program of urbanization brought about in Europe and in America deep transformations of the urban fabric. This program was deeply influenced by architectural functionalism, and strongly linked with a particular vision of the world and society. In general, architectural problems took precedence over the urbanistic, with the result that some fundamental questions were clarified, while others were overlooked. That careless attitude toward urban phenomena was, during those twenty-two years, detrimental to the homogenous development of the urban activities in Europe as in America.

In Germany, in the first twelve years after World War I, the dwelling was felt to be a symbol of an ethical nature. The home and the neighborhood were at the center of a moral imperative to determine the balance that was operating from the interior of the cell where man lives, and to achieve the sublimation of all social contrasts in the rediscovered coherence between function and form. The house was at the base of a new experience of living in relation to well-determined and constant functions. It was an expression of living in the perfect organization of the different parts, according to needs that were to be the same for all men, collective needs (living rooms), individual needs (sleeping areas), or complementary needs (utilities). The measures were made as perfect as a key fitted in the functional dimensions of the different activities of life.

The very rigorous analysis of human behavior did not produce totally industrialized prefabrication, as was the dream; but the multistory dwelling, the row house, and the duplex belonged to a well-defined schedule that eliminated all the former building-type definitions. The street was precisely calibrated according to the traffic, the building became free from the limitation of the street, and the neighborhood became defined by contrasts — a fact that well justified the linear form of the building in a figurative disposition of pure volumes. The method of the natural sciences seemed the readiest way to reduce all the deductions to one dimension. Yet it involved a preconception that has proved one of the most dramatic illusions of functionalism.

The idea of the neighborhood built according to a logic of systematic reasoning, with forms conceived as an immediate translation of the values of the life to be lived in it, the belief that the technology could promote harmony between social classes, independently of any political process — these are the result of an overhasty embrace of theories without the necessary if laborious preparation of the inductive description of different observable facts. Indeed, the functionalism of the twenties proposed all over again, though in different terms and without his romanticism, the social objectives of Ebenezer Howard.

Functionalism developed in a revolutionary situation, and it consequently denied any perceptible significance to the individual facts of history. From the "idea" of the urban environment every individualizing expression was carefully excluded (at least in the theoretical formulations). The real concern was the creation of an ideal framework for the typical man — something from which we are not yet immune. Characteristically, the limits of functionalism became evident in its inability to cope with the great human migrative problem. It was seen in the indifference toward the great urbanistic problems of an enlarging world, an indifference that was related to the spiritual tension of those twenty years, a pause of anguish in man's search for a more stable limit, which was an attempt to deny or hide the fear of a future whose opening was so close at hand. Technology was idealized in order to define a concrete image in a functional continuity.

The concept of the "new city" was determined by a need for something technically and functionally unified. The search was for an expression in just opposition to the plethoric chaos of the existing city, for something that could make a program. The new city of the functionalist received various visualizations, some of a technicist character, others poetic (Le Corbusier), but all seeking to define reality in formal terms and therefore much concerned with the exterior aspect of the urban space. In La Ville Radieuse form is given to a world of poetic perceptions, and imaginary aspects of the city movement are raised to a new power with intuitive indications of plastic values; yet the situations that are created so dramatically by this ideal urban system tend to be overlooked.

The utopia of La Ville Radieuse is quite different from that of Owen and Fourier because the latter, although they were detached from the circumstances, were engaged in the reasons for the social changes. The planners of the ideal city in the thirties, on the other hand, were generally indifferent to the experience gained over so many years by observation of the city from within — experience laboriously collected in a century of building transformations and social change. Indeed, it has been a fortunate circumstance that functionalism did not bring substantial alteration in the urban fabric and that no serious interruption occurred in the internal development of the city core. Such an interruption would have seriously jeopardized what functionalism did on the general cultural level.

In England, as in no other country, urban planning received a dimension and a rhythm of realization involving the structural transformation of the city and region. In many ways planning in England is a demonstration of technological power and of its influence on new social activities. A proof of this is given by the widespread reaction to its effects and the rather hasty repudiation of the formal character of some of its manifestations.

The idea of the New Towns brought to the general principles of modern urbanism a real revolution, the consequences of which it is probably too early to judge. In the ample critical material dealing with them, we can detect two attitudes toward the New Towns, one positive and one negative. Two different sets of criteria developed. One was based on the lack of relationship between programs and realization. It was a condemnation of all the measures of compromise that somehow affected the original program and its functional development — a criticism of a technicistic nature. The other is expressed as an aesthetic judgment; its proponents point out the formal shortcomings of the New Towns by observing that excessive decentralization took away from the city that wholesome civic life which every urban structure should maintain, and of which tradition gives us so many significant and varied examples. Both kinds of criticism lack a proper foundation because both judge the city as it is, without questioning the actual programming where diverging concepts may be found at the start.

In reality, the New Towns policy radically changed the character of English society with the realization of a new class equilibrium and with the technological organization of labor as a new pivot for national life, an expression of a developing productivity. It has been the greatest revolution in Europe in the last twenty years. Obviously, if one lives inside the phenomenon, one is bound to exaggerate the importance of marginal mistakes within the general achievement.

One criticism has been that since a city is always a phenomenon of concentration, the contemporary diffusion of the city does not make sense either from the human or from the historic standpoint; therefore, it is argued, we must go back to concentration, which expresses the perennial sense of the city. Such criticism of the New Towns calls attention to the excessive dispersion of the building fabric on an unqualified space because the continuity of the building masses is interrupted. As a consequence, a great deal of analytic study of the details of urban furniture, street signs, show windows, skylines, green areas, seats, and benches forming a reasoned ensemble of emotional ties, was carried on — all in the vain effort of defining a new kind of emotive-psychological relationship between man and environment. Some of the English New Towns furnish the best proof of the inability of our generation to build an urban fabric at once really new and really expressive of a full civic life.

The Greater London plan retains the traditional concentric scheme of the city. In fact, it was selected by its authors because it did not depart from the traditional scheme, traces of which were evident in the thirteenth century. The scheme contains innumerable groups of settlements that are co-ordinated with the larger form, so that a plan respectful of the traditional urban configuration appeared possible in order to co-ordinate again the old and new settlements. In the case of London, then, we have a situation with no middle terms, with a precise direction, the direction that will be followed on a national level and that may be summarized as follows: (*a*) as much respect as possible for the unchanging traces of the existing aggregate, (*b*) exposure of the great parameters of general planning to the most advanced ideas concerning the changing of a structure.

In other words, here is a scheme on a national level that may be revolutionary in idea but is based on a capillary structure whose consistency may be transformed with the plans. The form of the plan of London is, no doubt, one of the reasons that the city rose from its ruins preserving its characteristic image, particularly in the central zone, along the bank of the Thames, and in other areas so rich in historical meaning. The linear form of the MARS plan would have involved a radical departure from the pattern, frustrating its authors' attempt to keep the same center for the city.

Smithson's plan for a comprehensive community with the possibility of change led to an ideal concept of a road pattern that is roughly a triangular system. This allows one decision to be taken at each junction and a density of the land to be established in relation to the size of the triangulations. The tendency is in the direction of the clustered city versus the pyramidal. In this scheme, there is the powerful attraction of a single answer. In dealing with Soho in particular, a belt defines an area intersected by a system of linear shopping buildings, with parking and service roads and travelator levels and concourse.

The student who looks at the totality of urbanistic activity in England in recent years cannot fail to recognize that among the Europeans the British are the leaders in the concrete development of planning. The decentralization toward the New Towns, the plan for Greater London, the regional plans — these are all in the first stage of realization. After 150 years the same phenomenon places England once more in the lead of a social and economic revolution.

While the plan of London is linked with the total restructuring of England and has gone far to co-ordinate the major variables of a greater urban dimension, almost the opposite is taking place in the formation of a Greater Paris. The plan does not establish precise limits and bounds, but it rests on general criteria of the co-ordination of norms necessary to decentralize many industries and localize urbanization in an interdependent relation.

The London plan is helped by a lower density and a better system of communications, while the development of the Paris urban agglomerate extends today in the second ring of the Banlieue, which includes more differentiated and less dense residential sections than the older ring. In fact, many residential structures grow outside the Banlieue. They are high and immensely long buildings, typically of H, L, or M plan form, which bring a new dimension to the urban scene and represent the measure and direction of the process of urbanization of the Parisian region. Being conceived on a daring scale (the buildings are sometimes miles long), they enclose very large open spaces and are able by their powerful presence to co-ordinate the existing buildings and future growth around them.

It is usual to see the influence of Le Corbusier here. And superficially such buildings may not appear to be too different from many similar low-cost buildings in Europe and in America. But looking more closely, one notices a real internal strength that develops from their complexity. They have a strength that is not dependent so much on the size of the buildings as on their configuration, their brutal formal appearance, the loud chromatic scale, the impact lent by their prefabrication. These qualities make them very different from their European parallels — the celebrated well-groomed Swedish examples no less than the British, conceived sometimes with the stiff collar of modernism. The work of Candilis, Wogensky, and Vedres is testimony of that.

It seems clear to me at the present stage of urbanism only the strong ideas that are incidentally suitable for rapid realization offer valid alternatives to the unchecked growth of the urban fabric and its multiplying activities. Let us not forget the lesson of the strong, determined forms — the *cardo* and *decumanus* of the Roman towns or the squares of Philadelphia. They are still there, an unequivocal framework for the future of the city.

As significant as the powerful spatial figurations that characterize the new French building complexes is the methodical insistence upon distributing them everywhere. It seems the result of a cardinal logic that its culminating monument should be the unified complex of Le Havre. Let us not forget that Le Havre is a luminous example of communal solidarity: each owner's property corresponds, to the last square inch, to what he held before the destruction of war.

The future of Paris would seem to be the same as that of London. The city is partitioned into two distinct sections without that space continuity which justifies their integration in a vital sense. From this point of view, American cities are in a better situation, for a spontaneously spatial continuity was often created — as in Philadelphia the sequence from Independence Mall to City Hall, the Art Museum and Fairmount Park, or City Hall to the University of Pennsylvania to West Philadelphia in another direction.

The quest for the spatial continuity that may be obtained in the clustered city as well as in gigantic structures may send us back to Le Corbusier's Saint-Dié, where eight residential units would have been sufficient to house 20,000 people each. This was an absolute system and an absolute spatial representation, as in a work of art. Now, as you know, it is difficult to live in a work of art, and so the citizens protested: "You are not going to let us live in barracks!" But when the French architects employed the same criteria, they somehow made the results acceptable to the community. They have been able to develop for the city dweller a new dimension: a new urban realization as a mature reality for a community. They conceived of the city as a structure to live in, rather than a framework for other things, such as movement.

Two cities give a measure of the commitment achieved in the area of urban planning: Rotterdam and Amsterdam. Rotterdam (the world's third port in size) had to go through the total rebuilding of the central area; probably it is a case of missed opportunity. In Amsterdam the direction of development did not substantially change from that given by plans elaborated before the war, as the result of an optimistic attitude that said that since the place worked, it would keep on working. This, of course, could be true only of an extremely stable social structure, as is the Dutch community.

The finished product, the wonderful balance between industry and residences that characterizes the new neighborhood, is technically perfect. However, it is far from being a positive or satisfactory solution if creative value (which is the final criterion in urbanism) is taken into account. On the contrary, it is proof that an urban dimension is not created from postulates or from a figurative conception tied to it. It is through the assimilation of the vital qualities of the area where action is needed that an idea becomes creative and susceptible to being translated into structures that reveal the character of the contents.

Take the case of Amsterdam, for example. The cutting of the New North Canal, an event of extraordinary importance that could have lent great meaning to the structure of the community, has been joined to the realization of a plan based on the narrow integration between industrial and residential areas. The reconstruction of the center of Rotterdam has been so often criticized that it is not necessary to do so again. How unconvincing the criteria of the urban plan are is demonstrated by the deficient performance of the architecture, the buildings being given the form of exhibition stands aligned with no sense of their relative importance.

On the other hand, the additive growth of autonomous residential unities of 10,000 to 20,000 people, each subdivided into minor nuclei according to the rules of classic urbanism, is even less persuasive. Twinstad Zuidwirk, south of Rotterdam, is typical. To a perfectly calculated technical and functional operation, an arbitrary spatial distribution has been given. And because of the great extension of the unit, it appears to be disconnected from the reality of a more comprehensive urban development.

Confining this survey to Europe, I have not mentioned Chandigarh or Brasília, the two capital cities built in our generation. They are the two extremes of our time. "Chandigarh is an idea of life created out of life itself." In Brasília, "technology makes man act wisely and correctly, not by religions or ethics, simply by technology." Between these extreme positions one must be found for the urbanist as the architect of the city involved in its total experience. What already exists is valuable. If we believe in the validity of the human aggregate, the existing is as valuable as the new as a guide to directional capabilities.

Movement is the horizontal and vertical framework of the city; but it is only a framework, and the picture is within that framework, more important, more determining, more worthy. Buildings and city structures are becoming larger because more people work together, not because of movement. It is upon the human context that we must focus our continuous attention. The reality is there, the reality that changes things, destroys and renews them. The problem of movement is a technical one, and the better the solution, the better for us all. Multiple and simultaneous movement, however, does not represent and is not really sufficient to express the city. It is still where man wants a forty-foot ceiling that the representation of the civic space takes real physical form. It is there that the gamut of architectural expression, in its richness and complexity, is to be sought. To quote Edgar Wind, "We cannot solve our problems, even in art, by pretending that we act as primitives, for the gate of that old paradise is shut; we must look for a new gate at the other end."

The Baroque city, basically a cluster city with orchards and farmland in between groups of buildings, was generated from the interior of those buildings. The inner space modulated the walls, made a vertical continuum through the grand staircase, penetrated into the shade of the vestibules and colonnades; it extended into the open and elaborated the immediate surroundings of the building. Finally, its centrifugal force created the spaces of the city. That seems to me the reason for the extreme vibration of the Baroque structures, the decoration of the interior being carried outside into the Piazza del Popolo, the piazzas of S. Ignazio and St. Peter's.

It seems to me that we live at a moment where a reverse of the Baroque situation is being created. Cities will be bigger and fewer, but their character of shelter will increase rather than diminish. A dynamism of universal scale connects cities in a gigantic vortex. Our perceptions are now conditioned to this scale of movement, which is created because of the urge to live. This movement, the movement of our time, resolves itself first through the highways and the air, then in the fractioned rhythm of the civic spaces and in the large and continuous structures that will enclose so many activities. It resolves itself finally in the architecture, which must be immovable, a reminder of valid things in life, bigger than ourselves.

The stillness of the heavy structures, of the great spans, of the filtered natural light, contrasts with the light and ephemeral structure of the exterior dynamism where movement occurs. It is the experience of interior space that is still the peculiar phenomenon of architecture; this is what unifies the social content, the technical means, and the expressive values on every level, from poetry to prose, from the beautiful to the ugly. The interior space will be always the locus where all the manifestations of architecture qualified themselves and are applied.

The building becomes the formative element of the urban structure, its interior space the place where the human dimension is re-established, where the urban dynamism is resolved.

It has been said that the architecture-urbanism relationship is a quality-quantity one. When this relationship becomes one of quantity or scale alone, then the distinctions between architecture and urbanism, between specialized task and artistic individuality, will disappear.

Education for Urban Design

Origin and Concepts of the Harvard Program

JAQUELINE TYRWHITT

The term "urban design" is used at Harvard in quite a limited and specific sense to mean an area of interaction between the three professions of architecture, landscape architecture, and city planning, which are there housed together under the general umbrella of the Graduate School of Design. At Harvard we believe passionately that the environment matters. (Whenever I use the term "we" in this discussion, I mean the members of all three departmental faculties who are concerned with the programs of urban design.)

We believe that there is a positive value in the uplifted feeling one experiences on a marvelously fine day or in a really beautiful environment. This is not to say that the fine day or the beautiful environment themselves induce "happiness," but it does seem that a sense of personal well-being — of optimistic purposefulness — comes more easily when the eyes are alerted by a lovely setting (take, for instance, Cranbrook) than when they are completely deprived of nourishment (take almost any other place near Detroit) or when they have to be deliberately closed against the environment (take the more strident stretches of Woodward Avenue).

This personal sensation of delight is one aspect — and one aim — of urban design, but there is another. This is related to social responsibility, to a feeling of mutual responsiveness and mutual interest in the environment. When such feelings are aroused, one can anticipate that the environment will grow richer and even more attractive with age, rather than slither into the kind of thoughtless decay we know so well. For such a feeling of social responsibility to arise there must be a very clear distinction between privacy and communality, between *meum* and *tuum*.

Restraints and Freedom

I have come to this conference fresh from the Harvard Commencement ceremonies, where humorous remarks were made concerning the President's traditional greeting to the graduating class from the Harvard Law School as men qualified to devise "those wise restraints which make men free." I would like to take this phrase as a description of the tasks and limits of urban design as we see it.

Privacy and communality — like everything else in our profession — are related to scale. The privacy of the bedroom contrasts with the communality of the living room, the privacy of the house with the communality of the housing clusters, the clusters with the residential sector, the sector with the city, and so on. In every case privacy means a desired protection from intrusion by unwelcome, incompatible elements, ranging from an inability to shield the house from intrusion by one's neighbor's children to inability to keep trailer trucks out of a residential sector. In each case the needed protection should be given by design rather than by legislation: the private areas should be obviously less suitable than others for the needs of the incompatible elements. The demands of privacy are probably more commonly understood and met than the less explicit needs for communality. But without this no urban design will last longer than the powers of its management. Expressions of communality without forced intimacy (that is, invasions of privacy) must also vary greatly with the scale and nature of the community, but we believe design should afford each man an opportunity to be recognized by his fellows on an informal, take-it-or-leave-it basis. This is the framework within which each man may exercise his freedom.

Scenes and Systems

Order and hierarchy — the wise restraints which make men free — are at the very basis of civilization itself. For it was only after early man had discovered a cosmic order in the heavens, which he could organize within a conceptual framework of sequence, frequency, and proportion, that the first high civilizations could arise in Sumer and Egypt. This cosmic order formed the basis of the first architecture as well as of the first systems of social and religious hierarchy. It is totally impossible for us to deny order as the basic premise of civilization, but our interpretation of the scale on which it should operate in order to "make men free" has varied from one culture to another.

In the Harvard program urban design operates on two scales: the conceptual system and the visual scene. The first is a frame of reference, conceptually sensed but not necessarily visually apparent at any one moment; the mile grid of the Detroit area might serve as a simple example. The second is directly concerned with what is physically visible at the human scale — in other words, with the design of variant elements within the conceptual system. We hope that both the general system and the detailed element are equally important, and a theme that runs through the Harvard programs is that the designer must always be simultaneously conscious of the macrocosm and the microcosm.

Knowledge and Awareness

Now I approach the subject of this conference: in what way is urban design welded into the teaching of architecture and planning? But I must first remind you of the sharp distinction between knowledge and awareness. We all know that giving a professional training is something very different from opening up a field of general understanding: for instance, engineering is not taught to architects at a professional level, but the architect is, one hopes, made aware of the principles upon which the engineer bases his calculations and is given a frame of reference within which to operate.

At Harvard we have two programs in urban design that fall into the awareness field and one that is strictly professional. We endeavor to expose all incoming students — whether they are entering the program of architecture, landscape architecture, or city planning — to some general principles of environmental design. This occupies studio periods throughout the first term in the Graduate School of Design. After this initial term of joint work, designed to give an intelligent awareness of the interaction of man and the physical setting of his daily round, the students are plunged into the technicalities of their separate professional fields.

Ostensibly, those who wish to do so have at least one subsequent opportunity for collaborative work on an urban design problem, but this has become less and less practicable to organize. Each of the professions tends to lay increasing value on high standards of specialized *expertise*, and the gap between the architect's training in the technicalities of constructing buildings and the planner's training in the technicalities of decision making continues to widen. As a result, both enter their professional life further apart than they were on their entry into the school. One may deplore this, but it is difficult to combat it without lowering professional standards or lengthening the training programs.

Another, more mundane, reason for a reluctance to embark on collaborative programs is the great difficulty in maintaining a consistently high level of interest on the part of both the architects and the planners participating. The planners feel that it is superficial to move into the design stage without a far more thorough study of certain elements, while the architects feel that further detailed statistical analysis will not uncover anything that will materially affect their design. Whichever line the faculty decides on, one group tends to lose interest and work halfheartedly or else contract out and pursue an independent path. Several efforts have been made to deal with this inevitable situation, but all more hopeful solutions are difficult to program within an already tight educational schedule.

It was partly a realization of the inadequacy of collaboratives that caused the Harvard Urban Design Professional Studio to come into being. This is, at present, a one-year course designed simply to give further training to qualified men to help them fill the gap between the planning program prepared by the city planner and the building plans prepared by individual architects. It does not attempt to substitute for either. It accepts the fact that a dangerous gap exists which neither profession is at present being trained to fill. Thus the Harvard program in urban design does not aim to train architects in city planning or city planners in architecture. In principle, it adopts a planning program that has already been developed, and works on its interpretation in terms of three-dimensional design. If the planning program has set up a system, this is also adopted; if not, then a system must be evolved that will interpret the principles laid down in the program.

The next step is to develop tools for the shaping and organization of the urban scene; in other words, measuring units for the various elements of the plan. The purpose throughout is to develop "those wise restraints which make men free" and to create a framework to guide but not inhibit those individual architects who, it is assumed, will normally carry out the final work, much as the conceptual system, derived from the planner's program, has guided the urban designer in making his plans.

In addition to his major studio course, each urban design student attends a special seminar that continues throughout the year, as well as one or two elective courses in a department of the school or in another faculty of the university or at M.I.T. These elective courses are selected with the help of the instructors. We try to see that not more than two or three students attend the same course, in the hope that a wider range of general awareness will thus rub off on the group as a whole.

Students entering the Urban Design Studio must already be fully qualified in one of the three professions and must satisfy the admissions committee of their ability as designers. This is perhaps the chief difference between the Harvard program and that of some other schools. But, as I have said, this program is not thought of as an alternative to a program in the planning department. It is a deliberate design training in a field not covered in the regular curriculum of any of the three professions.

At this point, I should like to summarize two programs, one for entrants to the Graduate School of Design, the other the one-year Urban Design Studio.

One-Term Program in Environmental Design

The fall-term program of the first year in the Graduate School of Design falls into three phases: a general visual reconnaissance of a given area; a period of abstract research into general factors thrown up by this reconnaissance; a rather longer period of moving from a sketch plan to a three-dimensional model, and finally to a carefully drawn two-dimensional plan for the original area. Last fall a study was made of East Cambridge, and the reconnaissance program included events and their visual repercussions, relative scale of buildings and land use, photographs and drawings of specific qualities and features, and comparative studies of the nature of urban spaces.

These and many other subjects are discussed and analyzed in class as a basis for undertaking library research into a number of topics, such as factors that influence apparent scale, view, privacy from sound, communality of view (distances of recognition), walking distances, and size standards for street furniture. All such information is compiled on standard sheets, which are then used by the entire class as a basis for their subsequent work.

The class next returns to the area first studied and undertakes two exercises — social livability and analysis of problems and possibilities. They are then ready for the sketch plan, intended to show a system of design, and the three-dimensional interpretation of this system. At this stage the building types and their standard sizes are given; the exercise is in their placing in respect to all the criteria evolved as a result of the previous studies.

The Urban Design Studio

The Urban Design Studio presents two long problems during the year, one on a downtown urban renewal scale, the other on some new development in an open area. In addition there are some short problems, in particular an opening problem dealing with some area well known to the individual student. This gives us a chance to size up his interests and general capabilities and guide his subsequent work.

Last year the urban problem given was the Charles River Basin, taking as a basis the plans already prepared in the local planning offices of the bordering cities and universities. The second long problem was entitled *Intercity*, which was also the theme of this year's Urban Design Conference. The students spent the first few weeks analyzing, according to comparative scales, a great number of historical projects. After this, each student developed a system of intercity growth to suit his country of origin, and three were chosen for subsequent development by the whole class, each student at that stage acting as an urban designer required to work within the over-all system. The United States project group chose to work on an actual site along one of the corridors of the Washington Year 2000 Plan. The other two groups, for Western Europe and India, worked on an abstract, flat terrain within the geographic and climatic conditions of a specific region.

The faculty working with both the first-year studio and the Urban Design Studio are drawn from the departments of architecture and city planning. Their tasks fall into three categories: the provision of information, or at least the sources from which this can be gathered; a constant reminder that the designs have to be realizable in stages and by different people, because it is rare that a complete project can be built at one blow by one man; and a continual reference back to the macrocosm, the microcosm, and the reality — in other words, the system, the building types, and the special problems of the site.

The Urban Design Studio has now been operating for two years. Men graduating from it get a Master's degree in their own field with a specialty in urban design. This is a further emphasis on the fact that we make no pretense of turning an architect into a city planner, or vice versa, within this one-year program. But the program is still young. It will undoubtedly go through many changes before its curriculum becomes stabilized. We have learned much in these two years, and I believe next year's program will be the best yet.

THE WESTERN WORLD: A STUDY FOR A LINKLIKE SETTLEMENT *by Tjakko Hazewinkel* (1–3)

Design Intent:

a. Creation of an intercity settlement, which has a community life in its own right, but also stimulates the activities in the center of the existing main cities.

b. Mixture of all kinds of families: bachelors, families, and retired people. Mixture to a certain extent of social classes, a sound social structure being the aim.

c. Mixture as far as possible of the living quarters with community facilities. Endeavor to create intimate units of dwellings and yet a feeling of the whole.

d. Possibilities of growth and changes in the settlement structure, reservation of space for later development in the unit center.

e. Re-establishment of paved, citylike areas of high density as worthy human environment.

f. Educational, recreational, and transport facilities within walking distance for the larger part of the settlement.

g. Stimulation of the use of public transportation for commuting to work, etc. Acceptance of the automobile for every family as an attractive means of leisure-time use.

Habitat:

A great variety of dwelling types in a variety of prices; a high average of one-family houses with private gardens. Around the center: high-rise apartments. High-density region: gallery apartments in blocks of 12 and 5–7 floors (small and large flats and duplex apartments mixed up along streets-in-the-air) related with different kinds of one-family housing. Medium-density region: some walk-up apartments linked with one-family housing. Low-density region: private houses, linked together in a chain; patio houses, etc.

Work:

Near the unit center local firms can settle. The big working load nevertheless is supposed to be concentrated near the center of the main city or the new center for recreation and work.

Community Facilities:

The unit centers are linked to larger centers in two directions; comparison of shopping facilities guarantees sound commercial competition. In the center: shopping, restaurant, pub, police station, cinema, etc. Linked with the center: two high schools. In space for future development: junior college, trade school, hospital, some office buildings, some light industry, etc. Everything that enriches the liveliness of the center will be stimulated to settle there.

Theater, concert hall, department store, etc., will remain in centers of the main cities of new major centers of recreation and work.

Circulation:

Each railroad station (separated by one mile) services a population load of 54,000 inhabitants, living mainly within a quarter of an hour's walking distance from this station. Thus, cheap, rapid, and frequent transportation can be guaranteed for recreation and work. Car traffic is oriented to the highways on the outer side of the settlement. Near the unit center is a large parking area. All over the settlements are parking lots. Pedestrian footpaths interlink the whole settlement unit.

Open Space:

Units are bounded by large wings of green for communal use. This area will be occupied mainly by sport facilities intertwined with parks. Some public facilities may also be located there.

Inside every dwelling unit are small green areas for local uses (playgrounds). Near the elementary schools are sport fields.

Source: Intercity I (Cambridge, Mass.: Graduate School of Design, Harvard University, May 1962), pp. 28.1–28.4.

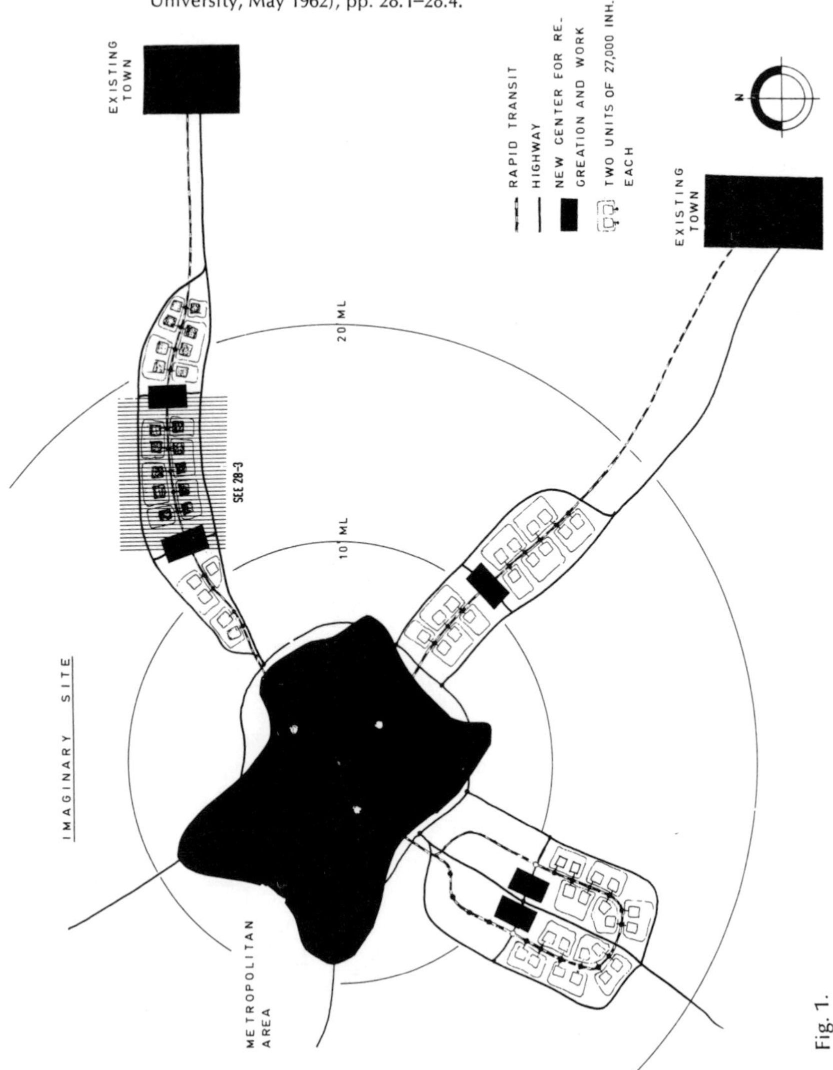

Fig. 1.

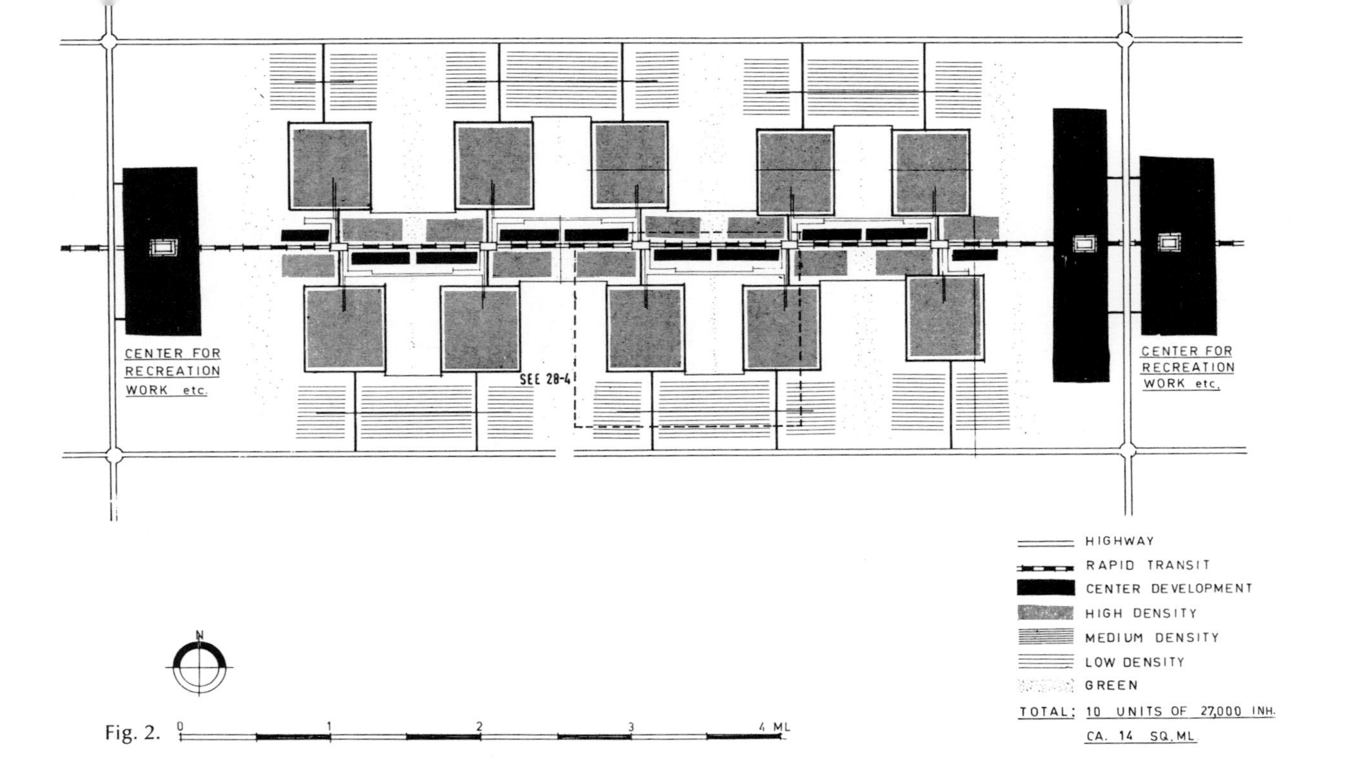
CENTER FOR
RECREATION
WORK etc.
SEE 28-4
CENTER FOR
RECREATION
WORK etc.
N
HIGHWAY
RAPID TRANSIT
CENTER DEVELOPMENT
HIGH DENSITY
MEDIUM DENSITY
LOW DENSITY
GREEN
TOTAL; 10 UNITS OF 27,000 INH.
CA. 14 SQ. ML.
0
1
2
3
4 ML

Fig. 2.

AGREAGE
ACRES
CENTER AREA 43
FEEDER ROADS 35
BUILT-UP AREA 514
LOCAL ROADS 32
PUBLIC PARKING 23
ELEMENTARY SCHOOLS 24
SEC. SCHOOL 13
OPEN SPACE includes: -sportfac. -sidewalk -promenade -parkarea -bufferstrip 206
TOTAL 890
LEGEND
RAPID TRANSIT
HIGHWAY
PRINCIPAL FEEDER ROAD
LOCAL ROAD
PEDESTRIAN AREA
PUBLIC PARKING AREA
GREENAREA + SPORTSFIELDS
CENTER DEVELOPMENT
MEDIAN DENSITY one family housing
LOW DENSITY car oriented one fam. h.
1. RAILROADSTATION
2. SUPERMARKET etc
3. PUBLIC FACILITIES
4. SPORTING FACILITIES
5. SWIMMING POOL
6. GOLFLINK
7 SEWERAGE STATION
8. HOSPITAL
9 JUNIOR COLLEGE
10. HIGHSCHOOL
11. ELEMENTARY SCHOOL
12. NURSERY SCHOOL
13. CHURCH
15 MIN. WALKING DISTANCE
0 500 1000 2000
N
5000 FT
1 ML
Fig. 3.

URBAN SETTLEMENT *planned by Mario Corea, Gustavo Munizaga, and Jan Wampler* (4–8)

Design Intent:

The city presented here is, first, a social form and, secondly, a physical form. The form of the existing city, with its miles of houses on quarter-acre lots, has become not only physically objectionable but also socially objectionable. It is the intent here to transform this bidimensional structure to a three-dimensional structure stressing the intercommunication of people at every level of living — in essence, to increase the urban social organization. The living unit, being the key element of a social organization, has here been the part most thoroughly investigated. This unit makes up only one part of the city, with the outside communication channel being utilized for activities to serve more than 45,000–50,000 persons. The places of work and education are attached to the communication spine. By providing higher density, more land is left vacant for the use of recreation activities. The conceptual order of social organization applied here has been diagrammed in Fig. 5 and represents the various places of social interaction or catalytic points. The concept extends from the home through Megalopolis and back to the second home.

The dictates of this intent thus make the city a region, which is composed of many different places instead of one place.

Habitat:

The city is composed of units of 35,000–45,000 persons housed in one building. Within the structure each individual is free to express the design of his house as he desires. The structure is a slab building 30–50 stories high forming a U, in the center of which are the local community facilities.

Circulation:

Five time and distance patterns form the basic movement structure of this project: (*a*) The ten-minute walk. Establishing the size of the container in which any point is no farther than this distance from the center. (*b*) The twenty-minute ride. A basic trip by mass transportation from home to work. (*c*) The 45-minute auto drive. A basic trip from the unit to extended points outside the linear development, i.e., recreation. (*d*) The two-day air trip. Intended for either business or vacation. (e) The seven-year move. A change of habitat.

In order to accommodate these patterns, various modes of circulation have been provided: Baltimore-Washington shuttle lines; mechanized movement from transportation spine to the unit; auto roads oriented outward from the unit; pedestrian ways from the unit center to the vertical access point (elevators).

Community Facilities:

Within the organization of community facilities five major catalytic points are stressed: (a) The horizontal street up in the living unit housing local needs, i.e., laundries, nurseries. (*b*) The community local center within the shape of the unit, containing elementary schools, churches, local shopping, etc. (c) The linear activity spine containing high schools, department stores, offices, etc. (*d*) The specialized places of work and education. (e) All major points within Megalopolis.

Work:

A series of specialized pools of work for industry, research, education, etc., is provided, along with the existing cities of Baltimore and Washington.

Open Spaces:

The most urban space is contained within the unit shape. The collective open space for group recreation is placed at the location of the high schools, recreation centers, stadium, etc., in the spine. The free open space of natural land and sea recreation is provided in tracts of land in a regional configuration.

Source: Intercity II (Cambridge, Mass.: Graduate School of Design, Harvard University, May 1964), pp. 3.29–3.37.

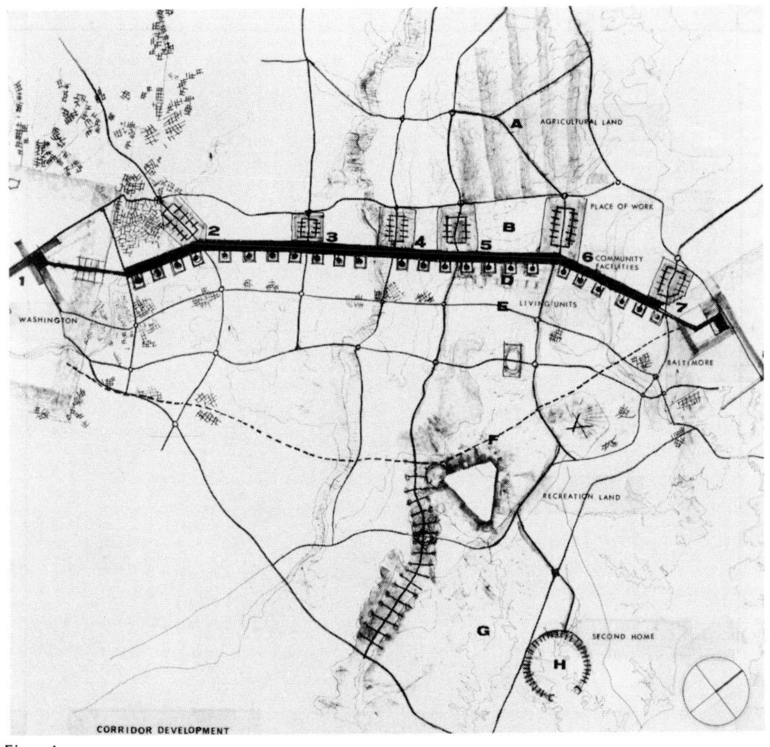

A AGRICULTURAL LAND
PLACE OF WORK
B
1
2
3
4
5
6 COMMUNITY FACILITIES
7
D
E LIVING UNITS
WASHINGTON
BALTIMORE
F
RECREATION LAND
G
SECOND HOME
H
CORRIDOR DEVELOPMENT

Fig. 4.

0 5 10 20
MILES

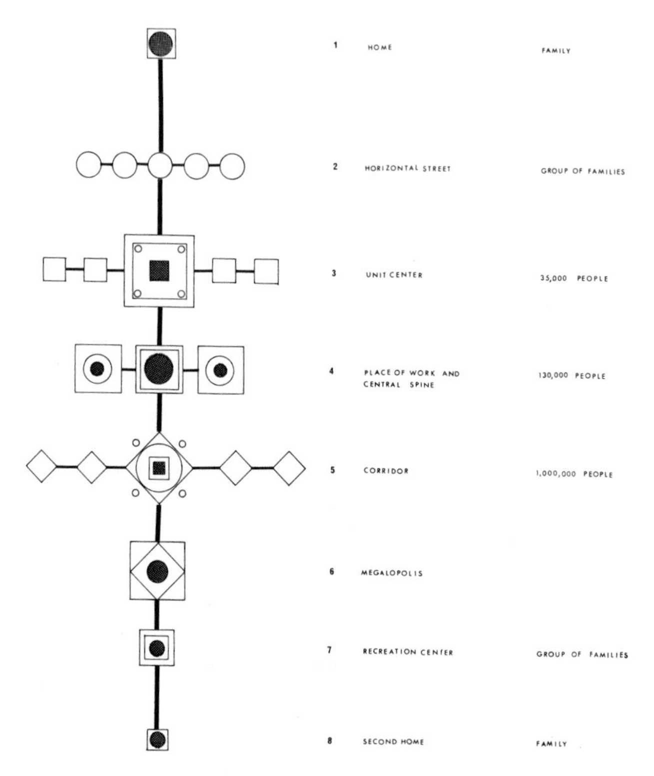

SOCIAL INTERACTION AT CATALYTIC POINT

Fig. 5.

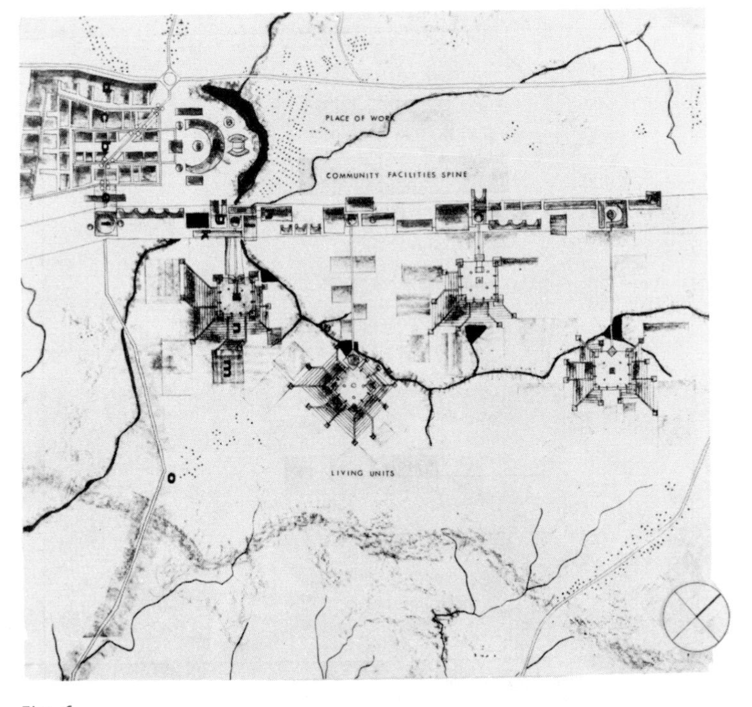

Fig. 6.

0 800 12000 24000
FEET

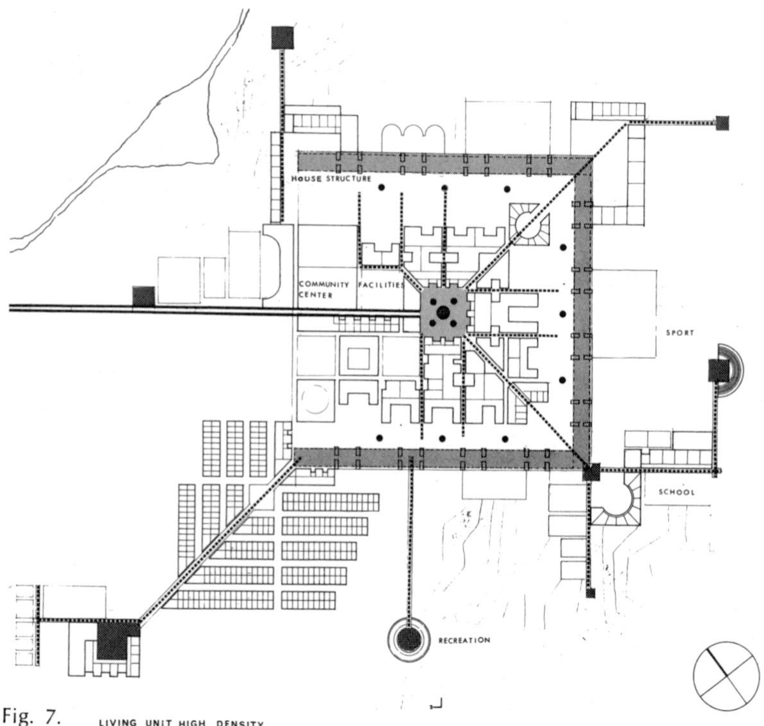

Fig. 7. LIVING UNIT HIGH DENSITY

0 100 1000 2000 3000
FEET

Fig. 8.

Design from Knowledge, Not Belief

The Need for Content and Tools in Design Education

BARCLAY JONES

The architect in this country today is a failure at urban design. One of the primary factors making for this situation is that the educational process in architecture fails to prepare the future professional to solve problems of urban design. What are the reasons for these two related failures, and what can be done about them? I shall try to explore these questions in summary fashion and raise some issues for consideration. I shall argue that the methods used in the past to try to remedy these failures will not work. We shall not succeed simply by trying to patch up our present curricula—adding a course here and there, changing the emphasis of this course, enlarging the scope of that one. Nor will any useful purpose be served by further castigation of the planning profession, or by reiterating that we architects *can* do urban design if anyone will let us. I shall try to show that we can remedy these failures only by drastically changing our ideas about architecture and its nature and our ideas about architectural education. These changes must be so great as to constitute a complete revolution.

The act of design, for the purposes of this discussion, is seen as a form of human behavior. Design education is a process by which we try to elicit desired behavior patterns on the part of initiates to the field. We can take the whole realm of human behavior and divide it into specific categories of behavior for various purposes that we may have. This is indeed what we do when we identify one kind of behavior as design. For each of these categories of behavior there are two important considerations: the similarities between the category and others, and the differences between the category and the rest.

An important breakthrough has occurred in the last few decades in our attitudes toward knowledge and the transmission of knowledge, or education. After many useful decades in which we tended to concentrate on the differences between various categories of behavior, we are now turning to concentrate on the similarities. In many fields it has been found extremely fruitful to focus attention on the commonalities a particular field shares with other fields. Developments in the thought of one field are transmitted rapidly to others. The advancement of knowledge that results is frequently startling in its effects.

Equally startling are some of the side effects. Scholars today often find it easier to talk to colleagues in other divisions of the university than to some members of their own departments who have completely different orientations. For example, economist A, a mathematical economist, may have little in common and find conversation very difficult with economist B. His closest associate may be an applied mathematician, C. City-planning theorist D seeks kindred spirits in managerial economics, statistical decision theory, and industrial engineering. His colleague, E, a planner interested in analysis, finds his friends in spatial economics, civil engineering, agricultural economics, and demography. The old disciplinary lines are breaking down in many fields that are changing. For instance, texts written for urban geography find their greatest use in sociology courses. In many ways we are reformulating the notion of a community of scholars.

Not all academic and professional fields have shifted their orientation from the particularistic to the common aspects to the same extent. Some fields are very conservative and have shown great reluctance to change. Others are more radical and have rapidly shifted to the new approach. To some extent the effect is cumulative. A field that adopts the new orientation tends to attract the more inquisitive and creative students. As these individuals enter the field, it becomes even more oriented to change; conversely, the more conservative fields attract the less iconoclastic recruits and continue to populate their professions with traditionalists.

Architecture today appears to be one of the most conservative and traditional of academic and professional fields so far as the recent revolution in attitudes toward behavior is concerned. Architecture continues to the present its ancient and venerable emphasis on the differences between itself and other fields. Design is taught as architectural design — a kind of human behavior different from all others. Most of the student's time in current curricula is spent in being indoctrinated in those things which differentiate him from all others. The spokesmen for the profession chant in endless litany, "The architect is a creature apart." There seem to be signs everywhere of a hardening conservatism of this sort. If these conservatives and traditionalists prevail, the result will be ruinous to architecture both as an art and as a profession.

The cult of differentiation can be referred to as totemism. Totemism is a kind of individual religion in which each unit, small group, or clan emphasizes its differences from all others by having gods particular to itself. In this sense architecture today is totemistic, and what we must have now is a revolution against this totemism. I shall try to indicate the nature of such a revolution and the means of carrying it out.

But first, one point must be cleared up. There is a great deal of confusion about generalization and specialization in architecture. Many of the people I have labeled as totemists, those who stress the things that are different about architecture, claim that the architect is and must be a generalist. If they indeed meant what they said, they would be stressing those things architecture has in common with other fields, and they would no longer be totemists. But what is usually meant by the statement that an architect must be a generalist is the grossest perversion in terms. It means he must be completely specialized in architecture and know nothing specific about any other field. It usually means that most of the student's curriculum is sharply focused on architecture and that he is permitted and encouraged to take only a very few of the most general survey or appreciation-type courses in other departments. It must, above all, be made certain that he never has a chance really to learn something or anything about any other field. This is pernicious double-talk.

It is the very nature of the revolution necessary in architecture today to make the field more general. Professional education must become more general also. But it must really become more general, not in fact more specific, while lip service is given to the development of generalists. We can become more general in a meaningful way only by directing our attentions toward learning what architecture has in common with other fields.

Creative behavior in all fields of human endeavor depends on two characteristics: (1) the ability to learn, to acquire knowledge, to receive information, and to perceive reality; and (2) the ability to apply our learning to the solution of a specific problem, whether abstract or practical, to synthesize, to solve, to create, and to design. Many fields are deeply concerned with creative behavior, and many academic disciplines are dedicated to eliciting this kind of behavior. In architecture we hold this in common with many other disciplines. We must find out what others have learned about creativity. We must learn about their methods for trying to develop it in their students. Some other fields have already obtained astonishing results.

If we accept the fact that architectural design has common aspects with other kinds of human behavior, then education for it develops out of the two characteristics previously described. First, the student must learn how to learn — not simply how to do what is already known, which is by and large the way we initiate him today. He must be given means by which to acquire knowledge relevant to a problem — any problem — and learn how to use it. He must start at the most fundamental level and find out what we know about the nature of knowledge, the process of acquiring knowledge, and the ways in which we apply our knowledge to solve human problems. Then in slightly less abstract fashion he must apply his tools to very general problems — acquiring relevant specific knowledge, realizing what this knowledge means, and using it to select a course of action. Then, and only then, he must proceed from this solid foundation, which he shares with other professionals, to those matters which are specific to his own field. Once he has a general approach to problem solving, he can learn to apply it to architectural problems.

The student progresses from the most abstract level to the most specific. This process cannot be expected to be very popular with students, especially at first. Students usually want to learn how to do things immediately, not how to learn about things. They also want the knowledge of others transmitted to them as painlessly as possible, rather than learn how to learn for themselves. Probably, it will be necessary to carry some of the specific subject matter into the introductory period so that the student can develop insights as to how the material will be relevant in later work. However, the present so-called case study method should be relegated to the end of the curriculum, if it is retained at all. New courses will have to be developed for the needs of architecture students. This means that the revolution can come about only through the reorientation of individual faculty members within architecture departments themselves. This is the hardest way to accomplish a revolution. It is also the longest and most time consuming.

Let us look more closely for a moment at the decision process. The creation of architecture as a form of human behavior has persisted for a very long time. The process I have described of acquiring relevant knowledge and applying it to the solution of problems of shelter has prevailed the whole time. However, the methods by which the process has been carried out have changed considerably.

The aspect of behavior that is the decision process leading to the solution of problems of shelter exists at its most rudimentary level in various forms of insect and animal life. Here the decision mechanism is biological and is built into the genetic equipment of the creature. Complex hives, burrows, webs, nests, cocoons, dens, lairs, and heaps are the elaborate results of these instinctive decision processes. Among the higher forms of animals these decision makers are replaced by others. The chief advantage of adopting new decision processes seems to be that greater adaptability and flexibility in solving shelter problems results. Nevertheless, serious penalties are involved also. More or less conscious decisions must be made entailing psychic wear and tear. The dominance of the higher animals suggests that the flexibility achieved is a net advantage of some consequence. Man lacks biological decision makers to a great degree. This gives him maximum flexibility of action in solving problems. It gives him the greatest flexibility of all animals in solving problems of shelter.

Through history man has developed several methods of approaching problems and transmitting time-tested behavior patterns that have accomplished successful solutions to the needs of people for shelter. Parents transmit the benefits of their experience to children, families to their progeny, and cultures to their descendants. Verbal and visual, conscious and subconscious instruction are used for the indoctrination process. Cultural patterns develop and become decision makers. Adaptations evolve slowly. Successive problems are solved with only minor modifications over previous solutions. As the decision problems facing the individual become more and more complex, and as division of labor increases, there is in society a tendency to create a class of specialists whose function is to make decisions relevant to the provision of shelter. Among the advantages of having a separate class of this kind are the superior training and experience that may be brought to bear on shelter problems, the detachment of the specialist who is seldom providing shelter for his own use, the possibilities of solving more complex problems by accepting delegated decision authority from a group of individuals, and co-ordinating group efforts toward the solution of a single problem.

As problems of shelter get more complex, it becomes necessary to develop a decision system appropriate to the level of complexity. Most of our recent struggles have been associated with attempts to replace one kind of design system with another. The important question is: What is the basis for any individual decision related to a problem of shelter? Histories of decision recognize three main kinds of systems: belief, reason, and scientific method.

Belief as a decision system requires the ritualization of as many separate decisions as possible. It breaks down when the number of ritual solutions to specific problems increases beyond the capacity of human memory. Memory then must be supplemented by methods of storing ritual solutions in writing or diagrams. Eventually retrieval from storage becomes cumbersome, and it is necessary to generalize and simplify the process. In many primitive societies today, and in some not so primitive ones, we still find an element of magic attached to the orientation of the dwelling, the pitch of a roof, the placement of openings, and the handling of certain kinds of ornamentation — hex signs, for example. Vestiges of this attitude can be found among laborers in the building trades even in advanced societies.

Reason and logic create an even more powerful decision system. Their application permits the development of much fresher and more creative solutions than the ritualistic approach did. More flexibility and adaptability are added to the system, and it is possible to solve rapidly changing problems with greater success. Spoken and written language, the printing process and photography facilitate the exchange of experience among men. Handbooks, perhaps, provide an example of this kind of approach. A rational or logical solution to a shelter problem becomes something of an ideal. Consistency becomes a goal in its own right. The development of a design philosophy by rational methods, and the application of it to a whole range of shelter problems in the work of a single architect, is itself an object of beauty. We speak of consistency, honesty, and truth. The supremely elegant output of brilliant careers serves as sufficient testimony to the advantages of using reason as a decision system in architecture. However, there is one serious fault with systems of this kind. It is required of them only that they be internally consistent and that they be true only to themselves. Reason is not necessarily connected with reality. A logical system may be complete within itself but not be related in any way to the real world.

Scientific method seems to close the gap between the real world and reason. Inductive logic is substituted for deductive logic, and empiricism becomes the order of the day. We learn to develop theoretical statements and generalizations from our observations of phenomena about us. Very powerful techniques for advancing our knowledge become available to us. Measurement, experimentation, and a whole series of new, more powerful, and more abstract, symbolic languages become tools available for our use.

Scientific method is being extensively applied today as the decision system by which solutions to shelter problems are sought. This does not mean that scientific method is being widely adopted as the basis for a new approach to architectural design. Architects are called upon to participate in only a relatively small proportion of solutions to shelter problems. In fact, the decision system in widest use in architecture today is probably reason. As shelter problems develop incredible complexity in our atomic age and our world of three billion people, reason as a decision system becomes an ever less powerful tool, more and more inadequate as a basis for solving shelter problems. Under these conditions architects must change and adopt a new decision system. Otherwise there is not the tiniest hope that architects will make any worthwhile contributions to urban design problems, given the present scale and complexity of our cities.

The process remains always the same: only the methods

change. The solution of a problem of any kind requires the acquisition of relevant knowledge and its successful application. This is true, regardless of the system that is in use. The differences between the systems are in the means by which knowledge is acquired and the methods by which it is applied in the process of synthesis. Parenthetically, it must be accepted intellectually that it would be possible to arrive at a given solution without any knowledge relevant to the problem itself, but the probabilities are infinitesimal. This is simply saying, in the classic example, if you seated six million monkeys at six million typewriters for six million years, one of them might produce *War and Peace*. For all practical purposes we can exclude the possibility of a design solution that does not proceed from a thorough understanding and knowledge of the problem and its related variables. The only question before us is: How do you acquire this knowledge, and how do you use it? Thus we are always designing from knowledge.

When an architect, as a matter of personal conviction, finally recognizes the fact that he must always design from knowledge, and when he also recognizes that the systems he has relied on in the past for acquiring and applying knowledge are no longer adequate to the problems that face him today, he is ready to reorient himself. He no longer finds himself alone against the universe, a figure out of Ayn Rand. He finds himself a part of a band of brothers who are struggling with exactly similar problems, in a general sense, in a wide variety of fields. He discovers he has a great many things in common with many others and finds in this commonality a source of insight and inspiration. New wellsprings of creativity are opened to him. For him, the nature of architecture changes, and many problems vanish. And unless it does change in this way, no contribution to urban design will be forthcoming. If we wish to train our architects so that they can participate in urban design and make creative solutions to the problems that face us, we must alter our educational system along these lines.

The first function of a designer is to predict how his design will work. Today this is not often fulfilled in architecture and urban design. We have reached the point where we are reasonably sure that structures will stand up. We can make predictions about the ways in which they will shed water, retain heat, admit light, and so forth. But as to whether or not they will prove satisfactory solutions to the complex problems of sheltering human functions, we fail too often to predict with any degree of certainty. The reason seems to be very simple. The complexity of the problems with which we are faced has far outstripped the powers of our decision system for solving them. This is particularly true with respect to urban problems. It is impossible for the human mind to comprehend the scale and complexity of a modern metropolitan area in the United States today. The numbers of individuals that comprise it cannot be comprehended. The differences of their natures, their activities, and their relationships are even farther beyond our capacities. A modern city is an incredibly complex thing. The most powerful tools available to us are not sufficient to achieve anything approaching a sophisticated understanding of these vast agglomerations. We are continually trying to develop new and more powerful tools to aid our understandings.

We have only two choices in trying to achieve the standards set by successful urban designs in the past. One of these is to make our cities as relatively simple and uncomplicated as they were a thousand years ago so that they are within the powers of our decision system to find solutions. The other is to accept the complexities of the world about us and to seek more powerful decision systems as a basis for our design. If we choose the first, regardless of the style in which we execute the result, the solution will belong to another period. There is no alternative to the second route to a truly twentieth-century urban design. A hybrid compromise is no solution. The best that can result is a cartoon of urban design like Broadacres or Brasília, or many of the student problems one sees. These solutions have much less relevance to urban design than the fake ruins built during the Gothic revival period in the eighteenth century had to architecture.

Urban design is not the monumentalization of some private

joke. It is the articulation, meaningful accommodation, and expression of the human relationships that are embodied in the city. If we would train urban designers, we must give them the tools whereby they can learn what the significant relationships are in any problem with which they are faced. In exposing the architect to these tools for learning, we shall also expose him to a whole series of other people who are acquiring the same tools for applications to their own problems. The architect will come to know and to understand others who are working with the city and its problems, and he will come to share their tools. He will also find that he shares the same tools with a host of other people who are not working on urban problems but many different kinds of problems. He will develop insights concerning the solving of problems from these others and be a more powerful designer as a result. The focus of the architect will change. He will no longer be obsessed in the same way with the internal consistency, purity, and truth of his own design. The design will relate to reality rather than to some abstraction. The solution will come out of the problem rather than be imposed upon it. The focus will be outward rather than inward. The problem will be seen as in a larger context.

Suppose we have the will for a revolution in architecture, how shall we implement it? We are concerned with two things: a new system of acquiring knowledge and a new means of applying it. First, we must ask ourselves who about us is concerned with the first of these problems. What have they found out about it, and what can they share with us? When we phrase the question this way, we see possibilities all around us. These range from philosophical attitudes concerning the nature of knowledge such as probability to methods of absorbing bewildering quantities of information in usable form contributed by mathematical statistics, to tools such as electronic data processing for rapidly handling, storing, and retrieving when needed great quantities of information that are too cumbersome for our meager minds. Many other developments can be found that are concerned with the nature of learning, perceiving, and acquiring knowledge also. Though they are somewhat more

problems? How do they structure them? By what means do they seek their solutions? How do they reconcile the ancient conflict of combining information and judgment? At a certain level of abstraction their conversation is the same as ours. The insights they have about these same problems are very helpful at times. I recently attended a series of meetings of industrial engineers. Here are some of the kinds of things they were saying:

Our powers of design are being restricted because too much of our designer's time is being spent on aspects of the problem in which there is little or no real choice, and, as a consequence, when he finally gets to the really critical design aspects he has not time or energy left for them.

Computer simulation is and always must remain an art.

In the application of statistical decision theory to the solution of problems there can never be any substitute for the use of creative judgment.

And finally even:

The manufacture of ingot steel is a black art which we can successfully analyze only to a limited degree.

The same basic problems beset us all. During the Depression there was a joke about a stock salesman who had been out of work for quite a while. His savings gone, he was desperate. Finally he saw an ad for a job in a carnival. He applied to the manager and said, "Whatever the job is, I'll take it. I'm starving." The manager replied, "Times are bad all over. Our orangutan died, and we can't afford to replace him, so we have skinned him, and we want you to sit in his cage in his skin and amuse people on their way into the show." So the stock salesman took the job and sat there scratching himself and eating bananas happily as the evening crowds filed into the tent. After a while he saw that the connecting door to the lion cage was open. Before he could close it, the lion came through. In panic, he climbed to his highest trapeze and clung there shuddering as the growling lion prowled around below. Finally, he could hold on no longer. He no longer cared whether he lost the job or not. He started screaming, "Help, help, get me out of here. I'm no orangutan. I'll be killed." Thereupon the lion looked up at him and said, "For God's sake, shut up. You're not the only stock salesman out of work."

Too often we seem completely convinced that the basic problems we are faced with in architecture are unique to us. But this is contrary to the experience of both life and art. There are many others groping with the same kinds of fundamental questions that are baffling us. It is entirely possible that some of them are having brilliant insights into the nature of these problems. Recent experience in many fields in which knowledge is shared and resources are pooled indicates that there would be great benefits for us from a similar kind of action. We must stop thinking of ourselves as unique. We must no longer conceive of architecture as a thing apart.

Finally, something should be said about the kinds of visual results that should be anticipated from the revolution outlined here, though it is probably not a very important point at this stage. The purpose of the revolution is not to effect a stylistic change. It is more fundamental. If a stylistic change were the goal, then it would be essential to describe the visual results that could be expected. It is quite possible that the new brutalism — or, as I like to call it, feral concrete — would continue to prevail. Whatever the stylistic results, the visual impact would almost certainly be less self-conscious than either the work of Simon Rodia in his towers at Watts or Frank Lloyd Wright in his Guggenheim Museum in New York City. The real results of the revolution would be more startling, but perhaps less visible, less blatant. The works of design that would result might be more neutral in form than what we are currently producing, but more extreme in content.

In any event, we would be given a basis for urban design. The designer would approach the complex problems that are the order of the day with a deeper understanding of the city, a better capacity for acquiring knowledge relevant to the problem at hand, and better methods of applying this knowledge to the solution of problems. A more profound, a more truly creative solution would result.

Education for Designing

Questions Concerning Urban Design "Principles"

JESSE REICHEK

Architects and planners continue to carry, and educators in these fields to distribute, a bundle of outmoded notions and concepts that have been elevated to the status of principles. The new problems derived from other disciplines, as well as concepts of order and techniques for solution, are either unknown or ignored by architects and planners. We must seek to develop a visual-physical ordering from the activity systems with which we are dealing, even if such concepts of order demand a denial of those "principles" which we have been taught to accept as eternal.

So that there may be no mistake about the questions I wish to raise, let me state them at the outset as simply as I can. How many of the notions that we as teachers are guarding, distributing, and accumulating are meaningless, useless, and just plain wrong? Having accepted a physical determinist position, what evidence do we really have to justify this position? Do space, form, color, etc., really affect people's actions? If they do, then how and to what degree? How does the physical situation interact with other determinants? (I agree with John Dewey when he states that "the true purpose of knowledge lies in the consequences of directed action," and I should add for my part that knowledge is predictability.)

If the function of the architect and the planner is to provide a spatial system that will facilitate the process of activity systems, then how do our plans correspond to the operation of those systems in the real world? Are we planning or praying? When we examine the buildings and cities of the past, we find that they are derived from the prevailing socioeconomic patterns and the available technological capacities of the times. Are our notions concerning the ordering of our physical world based upon the present state of these factors? Or are we using concepts relevant to prior eras and attempting to apply them to present and future situations? There are many more questions that trouble me. However, those which I have stated are sufficiently general as to encompass the others.

Now that I have asked these questions, some of which may also have been asked by others during this seminar, I shall not attempt to answer them. Rather, I should like to share with you some thoughts that they bring to mind.

We who have been initiated into the mystic rites of design look at our cities and cry "chaos." Of course we except those portions of the city which we have designed. And about those, others cry "murder." We claim that our cities have no order, no structure. I say that this is not so. Our cities do have an order. That which is without order cannot be thought of or objectively seen. Where there is no order, perception and cognition are not possible. When we cry "no order," we are, in fact, saying that we do not know what the order is. Or if we know the order — which we almost never do, though we never admit to the fact that we do not — what we are then saying is that it does not please us, that we simply do not like it. In response to that kind of statement I can say that *I* like it. And where does that leave us? Whose father can beat whose father? The order of cities — any city, even Los Angeles — is open to rational understanding by the minds of men. I suggest that the architect, urban designer, and planner are seeking the lost paradise, the unity and order of simplicity, comprehensible at a glance, easily identifiable, and thus an easy way to one's own identity, having not the ambiguity of life but the specificity of death.

The systems by which we live either are of our making or exist in their present states because of the changes we have brought about in them. I think of one exception (and there may be others) — the solar system. It may be that before long we shall be bringing about some change there. These systems — biological, social, etc. — are open and interdependent systems, wherein action in one effects a change in all others. We of the AIA, ACSA, and even the AIP, have fenced in one sector of our environment — the physical environment — which we say is our area of concern and in which we are prepared to do good works.

The dictionary definitions of *environment* are: (1) "Act of environing; state of being environed," (2) "That which environs; the surrounding conditions," and specifically, "The aggregate of all the external conditions and influences affecting the life and development of an organism. . . ." These would include human behavior, society, etc. And so because of our desires and special training, we have chosen the physical environment in which to do our good works for the ultimate benefit of our fellow men. Since changes in our physical environment will come about willy-nilly, we wish to direct them so that they are more willy than nilly. In order to be more willy, we must act rationally. And in order to act more rationally, we have evolved a set of "principles" to guide our decisions.

I should like to examine some of these "principles." (The dictionary defines *principle* as a fundamental truth.) In examining some of these notions, which have been elevated to the status of principles by nothing more than calling them that, I should like to start with the most successful and end with the eternal.

To define the Greenway Principle, I quote the following:

The Greenway Principle is a basic linear system of connecting greenways, focusing on significant symbols such as churches, schools, and clubs, forming a skeletal backbone which gives significance and meaning to a series of individual projects, and provides a sequence of sensations for the people moving through it. It is a very humanistic principle that the community will be seen as a series of meaningful space sensations by the people who inhabit it. I felt at first that the application was limited, but I increasingly find that this approach to design forms a firm base for all other efforts.

Except for color, I fail to see how the greenways differ from the freeways. If either the color green or the trees have been established as a necessary element in the urban environment in order to bring about a happy urban life, I just do not have that piece of information. I shall lay aside the question as to their existence in the form indicated in the quotation. Freeways can and do all else that it is suggested the greenways do. They focus on significant symbols, perhaps not the same ones, though there are others of equal or greater significance they do focus on. But here I too am falling into the trap of using such expressions as "significant" without stating the significance.

Such terms as "meaningful space sensations" and "sequence of sensations" are nonsense without some indication as to what the meaning is and what the sense experience wants to communicate. Therein lies the rub, and therein lies the mumbo jumbo that we use to communicate to ourselves, our students, and the people we wish to serve. The environment, with or without the designer, is filled with space experiences, and they all have meaning. What are the meanings of the space experiences you wish to induce? What is the relation between this experience of space in the physical environment to nonspatial experiences in the nonphysical aspects of environment?

This notion of greenways is a device to achieve what we have accepted as one of the design gods: Unity. Our teachers have told us what their teachers told them, that we must "unify the composition." Since we are designing the Urb, and since every design must have unity, we "unify the composition." It seems not to matter that our present state of understanding of the Urb tells us that the activity systems for which we are to provide spatial systems are not composed states but process states. We are in constant search for unifying devices — building material, building height, street furniture, colors and textures, signs, architectural styles, etc. — as if unity corresponds to our real experience — mine, yours, or theirs.

There are other ingredients that we are sure a "good" composition must have — balance, rhythm, dominance, variety, scale, proportion, etc. By measuring and drawing, and in more recent times by the use of the 35-millimeter camera, we have been able to gather a whole potful of devices that we use to get "good" urban design. The list can be taken from any of the student projects at our schools or from the proposals of our more sophisticated practitioners. Open civic spaces (plazas, squares, parks) lend urbanity. Varied building types protect us against monotony. Distinctive communities give us our identity, and sharp boundaries our sense of place. Vistas — open and closed, short and long — as well as axial lines, give us the spatial experiences we need. Landmarks provide us with our orientation, both symbolically and physically. Pedestrian ways give us the human scale we want, the exercise we need, and a means of rejecting the automobile we love. (I hope you believe that we love automobiles. If you do not, I need only refer you to the most recent sales figures out of Detroit.)

We seem to accept these notions and devices as sure-fire ways of achieving good urban design for today and for tomorrow, even though they came into being as responses to very different patterns of life. We seem to ignore the fact that the spatial systems that have been developed and can be developed from them do not reflect or facilitate the activity systems that we are dealing with. Nor does it seem to matter that they inhibit the use of available knowledge and technology and strait-jacket us in our efforts to understand and adapt conceptions of order that have evolved in the sciences and in other fields of art.

Certain of our urban designers seem to have pets among these notions. Some feel that the civic open space is *the* device to use. The other devices are just not "in." The plaza gives the design that urban touch. There must be plenty of them, of all sizes and shapes. And we find them in miniature form in individual houses and in housing groups. There are those who hate cars and have used some of these devices to do the automobile in. The pedestrian must remain supreme. So the car is buried, walled out, collected at points, or regulated into extinction — they hope. Others hate people and have used these devices to harass them. For them the tree must remain supreme. People can go anywhere just so long as they do not use any space. Buildings may be put up anywhere, just so long as no trees are removed.

Some architects have a fixation on landmarks. They define a landmark as any building or object that was in place before they were born. They would wrap the city and any portion of the city around these landmarks. This, of course, would stimulate patriotism, pride in one's community, and a sense of place. Vistas, especially natural vistas, have a special importance to some. The values here have some vague relation to a sense of grandeur and the beneficial effects of an experience of great spaces. If, however, the vistas are closed, then the beneficial effects result from clarity of definition. Should the vistas be short, we are happier, because we have a sense of an intimate relation with our environment.

Recently we have those who are guided by the admirable objective of increasing choice. This is accomplished by cramming every conceivable building type, economic level, and ethnic group into each and every project. Hot off the press comes the plea for more diversity. This would be achieved by making it possible for one to go next door to buy a pastrami sandwich, ballet slippers, an abstract-expressionist painting, or water skis — all of which no neighborhood should be without.

In the meantime, the architect performs his task, which has been described as follows: "Architecture in Urban Design, then, is the articulation of space so as to produce within the participator a definite space experience in relation to a previous and anticipated future space experience." The architect is engaged in this bartending, mixing space cocktails, without having any confirmable idea as to the effects of his concoctions. He holds fast to his physical determinist position without producing any acceptable evidence to support his contention. I also have the hunch that the physical determinist position of the architect is supportable. But I am sure we shall be surprised once we are able to find out what, how, and how much. I have the further hunch that when we begin to find answers to some of these questions, we shall start to design spatial systems and provide spatial experiences that will have a real rapport with what we are and what we do and how we do it.

In more general terms, what I have just said is that we must be able to develop means of describing present events and predicting the outcome and prescribing the nature of future events. Each architectural design, urban design, and city plan is, in effect, supposed to be doing this. There are many who contend that we are using antiquated tools and primitive methods in attacking this task. We continue either to ignore or to remain ignorant of tools and methods that have demonstrated a great potential for utility. In like manner, we have disregarded important concepts of order that have emerged from the sciences and new patterns of order that have been revealed by our studies of our contemporary societies.

A word about Art and Science. Whenever "Science" is mentioned in a discussion of architecture or urban design, what seems to flash across most minds is: "What about the Art?" "Do you kill Art when you marry it to Science?" Or, "Art can never be pseudo-scientific." These and other like fears miss the point. All art at all times was concerned with and had an interdependence with technology and thus with science. I would say that art is concerned with the problem of ordering experience, and science with the problem of determining the order of experience. Thus the concepts that science uses in describing the order of events are of prime importance for art, which is engaged in establishing the order of events. It obviously follows that technology, which is derived from science, is inseparable from art. It is the means available for ordering.

Let me summarize. The "principles" that we have been using

no longer have any claim to being fundamental truths, since they do not relate to anything in our contemporary life experiences. The devices we have been using for establishing an order for our experiences are not in accord with the patterns of our lives. If the nature of our existence and the patterns of our behavior are pluralistic and ambiguous, what then is the validity of such notions as balance and dominance? When we are able to describe and occupy spaces that we measure in terms of miles per second, to what use do we put the notions of scale and proportion? And, indeed, what do we mean by human scale? Since our problem is to provide a spatial system that will facilitate an activity system that is diverse in its parts, equivocal in its structure, changing in time, and divergent in purpose, to what normative conditions can we possibly apply such notions as unity and focus?

We must stop rephrasing the problem to conform to our preconceived image of the solution and to be susceptible to manipulation by our ready stock of useless "principles." Our design decisions must be based upon concepts of order derived from the problem at hand. Design principles that have been formulated as a response to problems that no longer exist are irrelevant and detrimental.

hagen Metropolitan Area, where I spent the last year lecturing. This is completely astounding to the Danes, maybe less astounding to us, but it does give some indication of the nature of this problem of designing new space.

All went along well enough until Jesse Reichek came along and kicked the props out from under Perkins' plea by challenging the whole process of creativity by reference to the "mystic rites of design." He suggested that in our attempts to bring order to the apparent chaos around us, we may be praying rather than planning. His notion that where there is no perception of order, cognition is impossible leads, of course, to the implication that all concern with bringing order to the urban mess is nonsense. If we can recognize it as a mess or recognize it as anything, it has some kind of order that we are just not smart enough to perceive. He contends that there is order in everything if we could only recognize the system. It was probably well that Reichek came toward the end of the program. If he had talked the first day, and we had believed him, we would have had precious little left to talk about in this conference.

One of the curious things that happened, it seems to me, was the complete abdication of technology from a form-making role in the city. Everybody seemed to agree with Aaron Fleisher, who said simply that technology is not a determinant whatsoever. I am not certain whether he is right or wrong, but I suspect that one of the difficulties the scientists and the technologists have in the area of the city is that they are scared of the number of variables and the irrational concepts that we find there.

In one of the ancient copies of *Time* that I found lying around the dormitories, I noted a statement that, I think, bears out this notion of mine. It is a statement ascribed to a scientist who is involved in some of the far-out thinking in both science and space technology. He stated that he detests big cities and merely tolerates their irrationality. He was quoted as saying, "Nature is much easier to grasp because you can take a specific natural law and be assured it will repeat itself." Not so with people; therefore, the scientists, or some of them, it seems to me, simply withdraw and say, "Well, there is nothing we can do in this area of technology. We create technology, we make it, but we can't tell you how science will have an impact upon this rather curious thing we don't understand, the city."

We heard a lot of inevitable talk, of course, about the motorcar and motor traffic. I am glad that Reichek touched on this. I do not share his dislike of trees, but I do share his admiration for the motor vehicle. I cannot go along with those who say that we can solve our problems by turning our backs on one of the most marvelous pieces of machinery that we have been able to invent. The fact that we have not been able to be as inventive in the use of the motorcar as we were in making the machine itself is no reason for rejecting the automobile and sealing off our cities to it and saying it may not penetrate. Of course, the most obvious evil of today's city is motor traffic congestion, and it is true that on the day the internal-combustion engine was installed in the horseless carriage, the ancient form of the city that had evolved through centuries was doomed. Modern technology has produced machines that annihilate distance and make communications around the globe practically instantaneous, but it has not been able to solve the problems that the machines of transportation and communication have brought to our cities. These problems are far greater than the simple tasks of moving and storing. The motorcar has destroyed the ancient concept of the city as a social and political entity, and it has created in its place the urbanized region or "conurbation" (a term coined by Patrick Geddes fifty years ago when he foresaw this trend).

All of you know that we have currently under way in the United States the greatest public works program ever undertaken, the federal highway program, which by 1975, when it is scheduled to be completed, will have cost forty-one billion dollars. Half of the money will be spent in and around our cities. This is an unprecedented program of public works on a national scale, and yet there are few competent observers who believe that the highway program is going to solve even the problem of traffic congestion. In fact, there are many who feel that it is going to create many other problems. Even some of the most vigorous supporters of this program in Congress and elsewhere have no hopes that it is going to solve anything. It is a curious thing. Despite our valiant efforts to provide ample facilities for traffic through the federal highway program and other projects, there seems to be no hope that, in the end, traffic congestion will be reduced. Indeed, there are many who will say that when the program is completed in 1975, the congestion will be just as bad or even worse.

The automobile is an insatiable consumer of land. It has been noted that the Malthusian principle may be applied to automobiles, which seem continually to outrun available space. James Fitch of Columbia wrote an article in the *Columbia Forum* pointing out that no other form of wheel traffic has approached the destructiveness of the auto. Not only has the auto taken over the street, but it is dissolving all the connective tissues of the city. Most of us know that already two thirds of the downtown area of Los Angeles (if there is a downtown area in Los Angeles) is given over to streets, highways, and parking lots, and well over half the central area of Detroit has been absorbed by the movement and the parking of motor vehicles. Are we approaching the point where the automobile will take over entirely the central area of our cities, driving out everything else?

What can be said for the form and the organizaton of a city in a world that is changing so rapidly? I was fascinated by the schemes that Romaldo Giurgola showed. They are graphic representations of the kind of thinking that, I am convinced, we must get into. There is only one thing that I must remark on, and that is that we do not know what form the city will take but we can be quite sure that it is going to take a very different form from anything we are familiar with. I think that we can also be certain that the problems of providing form and organization to the city are so vast and so complicated that they require the concentrated attention of all the best brains not only in the fields of architecture, urban design, and planning but in a great many other disciplines as well.

We must take a fresh look at the institution of the city and translate its social and economic demands and possibilities into a rational organism, taking advantage of all the wonderful mechanisms and techniques offered by this age of technology.

At the same time, we must never forget that the city is for man, not the group man that you have heard a good deal about, but the individual man who still reacts emotionally and often irrationally to external stimuli. The city that we produce must be a fit environment for the spirit of men.

Now, if we are really doing anything about this, we have to start with first things first. I think that is what we have been struggling with a good part of the time here. It is an extremely difficult problem, and I was delighted to see this emphasis on what I would consider the fundamentals. It is my opinion that city planning has been suffering for many years from a constipation of ideas. City planning has been variously described as art or science or both. It must also be a philosophy. We have developed a competent breed of technicians who call themselves city planners, or a number of variations of the term. But where are the ideas? Einstein once remarked that "Perfection of tools but confusion of aims is a characteristic of our time." We have plenty of *know-how,* but we are short in the *know-what.*

I read another article in *Time* magazine some time ago dealing with advances in science and technology in which Edwin Herbert Land said:

> Discoveries are made by some individual who has freed himself from a way of thinking that is held by friends and associates who may be more intelligent, better educated, better disciplined, but who have not mastered the art of the fresh clean look at the old, old knowledge.

That is what we have been struggling with here. I also read a statement made by Dr. Luther Gulick, President of the Institute of Public Administration, in an interview with *The New York Times* a while ago. Dr. Gulick said:

> New conditions now require new thinking as a basis for new institutions and action. Some may think that our great need in the cities is water, or sewers, or wider streets, or more schools, or housing. Fundamentally, they are wrong. The real things we need are brains, character, drive, organization, and leadership.

What is the answer for the future among the people who profess the old-fashioned type of democracy based upon the dignity and the integrity of the individual? The fundamental question is: How much planning is consistent with the freedom of the spirit of man? Where is the point at which the right of the individual to do as he will with his labor and his life and his property must give way before the concept of the greatest good for the greatest number?

The welfare state is a fact in both Europe and North America. More and more the freedom of the individual is being restricted in the interest of the economic security of all and the attainment of social objectives defined by the majority. The submergence of unrestrained free enterprise may be unfortunate, but as the rate of urbanization increases, with millions crowding into and around major cities, there seems to be no other answer. Each of the faceless urban mob in a sense becomes, of necessity, his brother's keeper, and freedom of individual action must be circumscribed unless it becomes freedom to be throttled by the urban Frankenstein monster that we are creating.

We can put the question another way. (I am not giving you any answers; I am simply posing questions.) How can we organize our cities in their regional, national, and global settings, not as a bloodless, organized environment for bloodless, organized man, but as an environment that by its organization will free man from the oppression of chaos and furnish the framework within which he may enjoy his inalienable rights of life, liberty, and the pursuit of happiness?

Planners and administrators must never lose sight of the fact that we are not building our cities for the sake of transportation, or for fine and abstract architectural compositions, but for man with all of his prejudices and his convictions, his aspirations and his inhibitions, his irrational likes and his unreasonable dislikes — man, who still thinks and feels and who hopes and fears. If we are to preserve our civilization, we must find the ideas and then the tools to make the city a habitable place.

I am confident we shall find the answers to these problems, but it will require thinking and action on a far larger scale than we have been accustomed to. The problems that we face are vast and difficult, but I regard this as evidence of vigor in the city rather than of decadence. Growth in any organism is inevitably associated with disturbance and dislocation, and I would be much more concerned for the future of our cities if they had no problems.

The question of the implication of the points of view expressed during our sessions for education was hardly touched upon. I think that might be just as well. Any attempt to regularize or even to define a system of education dealing with imperfectly understood principles would be disastrous. Once we understand ourselves and our relationship to our environment a little better, we can talk with more profit about teaching and systems of education. There must be room for all kinds of schools and all kinds of approaches.

Only Holmes Perkins, in his keynote address, made a direct plea for the adjustment of the educational program in architecture by advocating a full liberal arts education as a prerequisite for admission to architectural school. This may be inevitable, but I do want to raise some questions. In the first place, I think that this tends to equate *more* with *better*. I do not think our liberal arts programs are very good now, nor do I think our whole educational system is very good now, and most of the answers that are proposed for improving our educational system seem to me to involve more of the same. The Perkins proposals also presupposed that the embryonic architect exposed to a four-year liberal education will become a better architect, or a better citizen, or both. I think it would be quite difficult to produce evidence to support this thesis. I am not impressed with comparisons with medical education. Among professionals, I think that doctors are probably the most self-centered, the most inward-turning, if not the most reactionary, group I know.

The assumption that there is some magic to free man's mind in some traditional areas of study in the humanities or the liberal arts may bear some examination. We might also examine the assumption that the humanities or liberal arts are broadening and provide a framework within which man may find his place in a world he never made. I suggest only that labels are pernicious and that some fields of study and areas of knowledge that are not ordinarily included under the humanities tent may be broadening or liberalizing or liberating.

I happen to believe that architecture in itself, approached not from a nuts-and-bolts point of view but from the point of view of attempting through a creative process to satisfy some of the ancient and basic needs of man, is such a liberating study. I can say only that two of the most "liberating" courses that I myself took as a student were both offered within professional schools: one at a school of agriculture and one at a law school. Both of these opened completely new vistas to me.

These thoughts about what we have heard are something less than a summation and, I hope, may be something more than a summation. I can say now to those of you who came to this idyllic spot to present papers or to participate so vigorously in the discussions only that I am personally grateful. I feel I have gained a good deal of knowledge and, I hope, just a little more wisdom. If each of you has similarly benefited to some degree, the whole thing has been worthwhile.

Index